On the Swirl
of the
Tide

also by
Don and Bridget MacCaskill

WILD ENDEAVOUR

On the Swirl
of the
Tide

Bridget MacCaskill

With photographs by Don MacCaskill

JONATHAN CAPE
LONDON

First published 1992
© Bridget MacCaskill 1992
Jonathan Cape, 20 Vauxhall Bridge Road, London SW1V 2SA

Bridget MacCaskill has asserted her right
under the Copyright, Designs and Patents Act, 1988
to be identified as the author of this work

A CIP catalogue record for this book
is available from the British Library

ISBN 0-224-03289-5

Phototypeset by Computape (Pickering) Ltd, North Yorkshire
Printed in Great Britain by
Butler & Tanner Ltd, Frome and London

Contents

Illustrations

7

Common seal with pup
Dog fox which hunted the shoreline
Large cub catches its own prey
Pine martens at a feeding place

between pages 144 and 145
Rainbow over Rock Point
One of Pinknose's cubs at about age two
Young dog otter, ready to take over
Injured otter, later found dead
Filming for television
An ageing Bodach foraging
Attempted mating – Palethroat and Bodach, afterwards
enjoying mutual grooming

Introduction

THIS IS THE STORY of Bodach, Pinknose and Palethroat, a family of otters who lived on a small West Highland sea loch in Scotland. It is also an account of two daft people who became so deeply interested in the animal that they spent more than a dozen years finding out as much as they could about it.

Episodes, recorded as they happened, have been condensed together into a period of about fifteen months in order to cover one complete breeding cycle and also to avoid a tedious diary effect. Each has been chosen as typical of many such occasions and each represents a facet of otter behaviour that helped to build a picture of the whole. With the exception of captive cubs observed within the holt, all were witnessed by either my husband or me, or both of us.

The otter has the protection of the law under the terms of the Wildlife and Countryside Act 1981 which forbids its killing and the disturbance of its resting sites, or holts. It is our belief that, in this crowded age and in so small a country, it is impossible to keep secret the whereabouts of any wild creature and that a more positive approach towards its well-being is to enlist the interest and support of the public. It is hoped that this book about the otter will help to do just that, and that the reader will wish to respect the otter's privacy and way of life.

If you are minded to try and watch otters, wherever you may be, go cannily and be sure not to frighten or disturb these delightful creatures or in any way cause them harm.

9

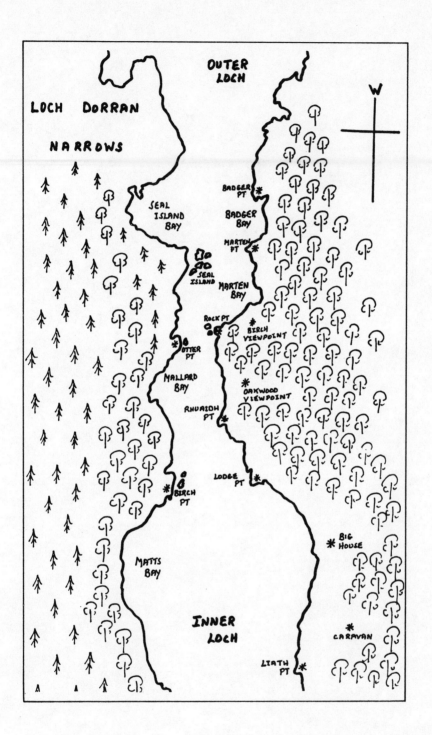

ONE

Secrets of the Shoreline

THE BIG DOG otter came gliding smoothly through the still grey waters of the Narrows with a wildly flapping fish in his mouth. A ripple on either side of him, fanlike, spread over the loch and faded away on its mirror surface. He dived into the tangle forest below and a trail of bubbles mapped his progress to the shore. He rose, majestic, from the shallows then, clumsy but triumphant, began dragging his reluctant prey on to a luxuriant carpet of glistening seaweed. In a narrow crevice between two rocks, he dropped it.

As the otter shook out his thick brown coat, all spiky with the water it held, a cloud of spray flew high into the air and fell as sparkling droplets to the weed. The lumpsucker, red belly bright against the dark weed, still struggled to escape. It was instantly seized. Crunch-crunch came the sound of otter jaws as wicked incisors went to work.

The misty morning was hushed to the sound of the otter's meal. Only the chirpings of small birds and the gentle lapping of the tide against the rocks were accompaniment to his appreciative munching. Now and again he lifted his head and was looking, scenting, listening for danger. Each time, reassured, he returned to his fish, savagely tearing a piece, chewing with obvious enjoyment, and gulping it down greedily. At last, only a few ragged pieces of skin remained.

He yawned prodigiously – pink throat and tongue and razor-sharp teeth for all to see. He stretched his long body and the muscles rippled down his spine to the tapering end of his tail. The

13

sharp claws of his hind feet, each leg in turn, tore fiercely at chin and breast, parting the fur and scratching it clean of sticky fish remains. Chin and cheeks were rubbed and smoothed over the moist tendrils of the weed. Then he rolled over on to his back and with wildly waving legs and squirming torso polished up his shoulders, back and haunches. He shook himself energetically and the thick dark pelt fell nicely into place.

The otter ambled over to a nearby boulder, sniffed carefully all over its weed-covered top, then deposited a dark dropping, a spraint that would tell other otters of his presence there. Then he trotted down the sloping rock and with no further ado breasted quietly into the loch. He dived. A rippled circle spread over the still water then was lost in the immensity of the whole. He did not appear again.

This otter was the dominant dog of the family of otters which we were studying. His name was Bodach, Gaelic for 'Old Man'. He was an old friend, and though 'relationship' was a term we would never use, he seemed to recognise our scent, was tolerant of our presence to a point and, so long as we kept quite still, would happily enough stay within yards of us for quite long periods. He had two mates, the bitches Pinknose and Palethroat. Both were more timid than he and more difficult to approach, especially when they had cubs. One whiff of our scent, too close for their comfort, and they would be scrambling over the rocks for the water. This family unit, together with its various progeny, were the chief characters in an otter study which we started more than a dozen years ago.

A small seed had been sown after Don told me of his one and only otter experience on Loch Dorran on the coast of the West Highlands of Scotland. He had been on a canoeing holiday with a friend and they had camped one evening on the shores of a narrow channel which divided the mainland from a large island. In the gathering dusk they had watched one of these animals lazily swimming through its dark waters. It had been diving for fish, eating whatever it caught from its paws whilst floating along on the current and, dimly glimpsed in the fading light, had vanished out of sight round a rocky point. The episode had lasted long enough to inspire a hope that, one day, he could see more of these creatures.

The years passed. We lived about as far as you can from the coast and most of our work was with the mammals and birds of the mountains, moors and woodlands closer to home. Apart from observing otter signs on river banks and lochsides we never seemed to find time to do more with the animal. One April, however, when we had a long weekend free, Don suggested a visit to Loch Dorran and I, still without ever having seen an otter, was delighted with the idea.

Loch nan Dobhran is the Gaelic name of the loch. It means 'the Loch of the Otters', but we call it Loch Dorran, in the anglicised form, which is much easier to say. We planned to camp on the large island known as Eilean Mor, 'the Big Island', on the opposite side of the narrows from where Don had seen his otter. To get there we drove some distance down the side of Loch Essan, a neighbouring loch of which Dorran was a satellite, and then took to the boat.

The 'boat' was an inflatable and too small for the amount of gear we loaded into it – two tents, cooking stove and fuel, food for two or three days, photographic equipment, sleeping bags and so on, the lot topped with our reproachful collie bitch Shian. It all looked distinctly precarious. There was a stiff north-westerly blowing and we spent most of the time baling out and hanging on to whatever next was trying to go overboard. While preoccupied with our hazardous passage, we caught brief glimpses over swelling waters and dancing white horses of an enchanting place – rocky shores on either side fringed with birch, oak and conifer woods and, above them, forested hills which climbed to high ridges, heather moorland and distant rolling clouds. All was sparkling fresh in the evening sunshine and full of the promise of an adventure begun.

As we neared our goal the sun was beginning to sink into billowing cumulus over a far-off ridge on the mainland, the golden orb transforming white cottonwool cloud into a pink inferno. Much closer the jagged heights of our island were starkly etched and savage against a golden translucent sky. Detail of the island was blurred. It rose darkly out of the still waters, mysterious in the gathering gloom and – to me at any rate – infinitely romantic. It seemed just perfect for otters.

'This is the place,' Don said with evident satisfaction.

We picked out a narrow channel, murky in the last of the light, its waters sluggish in the slack of the tide. Jutting into this channel and joined to the island by a long low spit was a large rock outcrop. It guarded a small bay. We edged through its shallows, bumping uncomfortably over rocks barely covered by the ebbing tide, then slid ashore on thick carpets of seaweed. Shian leapt from the boat with obvious relief and danced her way to dry land, but it was slippery and soft beneath our stumbling feet.

The spit, more or less level and with vegetation closely cropped by sheep, was ideal for the tents. In no time at all we had them up, one for sleeping and one for stores and photographic gear. They looked cosy and safe, glowing blue and brown from the lamps within. We had our first joyful meal in camp, always a pleasant moment but especially good this time, for in addition to the warmth of the hissing stove and the smell of a good fry-up there was the tingling feeling that otters might not be too far away in the darkness outside. We turned in as soon as the meal was finished.

In the morning, at first light, the dog and I went exploring. Don was still asleep. I crawled from the tent into a world clothed in mist, the craggy outline of the outcrop which sheltered our camp looming dark and almost menacing above. Its mysterious presence invited instant exploration. If the mist cleared there ought to be a good view from the top and there might even be an otter in the narrows below! Shian, trained to stalk deer and absolutely obedient, would not be a problem.

As I left the tent the spring turf felt good beneath my feet. Stealthily I groped through heather and soft banks of mist as we started over the great rock buttress. The dog led the way with her nose and would have got along much faster than I did had she been given her head. We followed little paths through the heather, seemingly too narrow for sheep, and I wondered if they could be otter runs, since some led down towards the water. I was making too much noise, though, and kept falling foul of half-hidden boulders in the heather and sending scree from bare patches rattling over the rocks. I was sure that soon all wild creatures near at hand would have discovered my presence and vanished.

Dewdrops glistened in the pale light and dropped to earth as we passed. The mist clung to the ground as if reluctant ever to depart, but as we scrambled higher the newly risen sun did battle with the pearly curtains and they were beginning to disperse. Soon it would be clear and bright.

The little path climbed steadily up and in a minute or two we were safely at the top. I found a sheltered seat in the heather which ought to give good views of the surrounding country. The air smelt of spring flowers and seaweed and the great boulders of the outcrop, the waters of the channel, even the heather, all were turning golden and pink in the dawn. The narrows, beneath sheer rock below, were shimmering in burgeoning light. I felt sure an otter would glide secretly through, unaware of its admiring audience above, but, for the moment, only a gull hovered on streamlined wings, lonely and calling mournfully.

Long minutes passed and the turgid waters slid by, unruffled by any breeze and apparently unoccupied by any living creature. It was a moment to savour, but it was an otter I had come to see. There were no otters. Breakfast seemed a good idea. I was just about to give up when the dog, lying quietly beside me, suddenly sat up, ears pricked and nose pointing. Something close to the water appeared to have caught her attention. I must admit my heart missed a beat. Lucky after all? Thumpings, rustlings, loud squeaks, and more thumpings came from somewhere beyond a monster of a rock to our left. It took only seconds for me to crawl quickly into its shelter and to peep round cautiously.

There were two otters, down on the rocks immediately below me, having an energetic romp. Completely unaware of our presence, they were scampering in and out of the heather, over and round the boulders, chasing, pouncing, nipping, kicking, wriggling, squeaking and squabbling. It was a romp to beat all romps, perpetual motion of seaweed-coloured bodies, and the sound of their whickering split the morning peace apart. My first impression of these creatures was that they were never still, and that turned out to be not far from the truth.

A small breeze began to tickle the back of my neck, and it was my undoing. Suddenly both animals froze to the spot. Two faces with small erect ears and inquiring eyes were briefly turned in our direction, then there was a startled snort and both were

racing for the water. Had they seen us? I don't know. But our scent filtering down over the rocks had evidently been enough. The last I saw of my very first otters were two small creatures paddling for dear life across the narrows to the opposite shore.

Having made a mess of it or not, I was absurdly thrilled by this experience. When I got back to the tent Don was up and ready for action; he too was delighted with the news that there were indeed otters here. While I put on the kettle for breakfast, he wandered over the shore of our little bay towards its other enfolding promontory. Exciting things might be discovered over there as well.

He returned in a few minutes, out of breath and obviously pleased.

'I've found a holt. There are cubs in it. I heard them squeaking!'

This was almost too good to be true. A lovely otter happening on the rocks right beside us and now the best proof of all that otters were on the island.

'Let's go back and have a look,' I said.

'Better not. I don't think the mother was there. They wouldn't have been making that sort of noise if she was. We might keep her away.'

It made sense. We decided to eat and then walk in the opposite direction to take a look at our island shore. We took the dog with us – Shian understood this game very well and her sharp nose could lead us to signs we might otherwise have missed. Again there was that tingling feeling of great things about to be discovered.

Loch Dorran was part of a wild and lovely region. The proof was everywhere about us now the mist of early morning was gone and the sun well risen. It was close to low water and vast carpets of seaweed, velvet soft beneath our feet, glistened wetly in the sunshine, bright green, yellow and orange, and many shades of brown. The shoreline was rugged and bordered with thin woodland of birch, willow and oak. Rocky promontories topped with heather and bracken stretched their protecting arms into the sea, and we guessed that there would be sheltered little bays between each.

Eilean Mor, with its tall cliffs and craggy tops, was a large

island, the guardian of two lochs, Loch Dorran and Loch Essan, and situated where the one merged into the other. Abruptly we were reminded of its more squalid history when we came across some roofless ruins and the trivia of everyday life – rusting cooking pots and bedsprings, broken bottles and jars together with the markings of lazybed plantings – forlorn evidence of cleared families driven to the very edge of the land by greedy flockmasters. For a while they had made a living on this lovely island but, in due course, were uprooted again and moved away to make room for yet more sheep. Ironically, these creatures were now placidly grazing on the fertile herbage round about us. They were doing well for themselves but little good to the island, for there were few signs of any regeneration of the trees which must once have been there.

We had separated a little as we continued along the shore, so as not to miss anything. I was walking through birch scrub and alder a little way in from the shoreline when I heard Don whistle quietly.

'Look at this!' he exclaimed as I joined him.

He was bending low beside a rock on the bank above a small burn which tinkled a merry tune, with small waterfalls dripping water into little pools at their base. On a large patch of sand where the stream met the seaweed shore there were the unmistakable prints of otter feet. The animal must have passed this way only a short time ago, for at high water the patch would be covered. We walked, one on each side of the burn, twenty yards or so up into the birches. In a short while we came to a hole beneath a boulder and there, on a bare patch of soil at its entrance, found a similar footprint. An otter holt, for sure.

Used as we were to looking for the signs and tracks of other mammals, we had no doubt about what we had found. As we wandered along the shoreline, inspecting the ground closely, we discovered more signs of otter use – secret holes that must be holts; padded down places with shell and fish remains lying on them; and, of course, spraints and secret little runs that wandered through the heather. Eventually we came to a great rock outcrop with huge boulders building to its heather top. As we climbed the steep rock from the shore a tangy fishy smell became stronger and stronger. It must surely mean the animal was only recently

here, and in some numbers – perhaps a family of cubs from a holt somewhere close.

'Look at that!' exclaimed Don suddenly, with evident satisfaction. He was standing beside an extremely large hole between two heather-covered boulders. It was overhung by a sheltering slab of rock with a small rowan tree growing beside it. The soil at its entrance was beaten down, as if heavy wet bodies had cemented it solid. A long sloping bank, completely bare of vegetation, fell away from the hole to a ledge below and was rutted, scuffed and smoothed. Cubs having a game? Chasing each other from one level to the other? At the end of the ledge we discovered another large hole, which also appeared to be in use, and we wondered if the two were connected below ground.

As we explored the whole of the outcrop we could only become more and more pleased. Otter runs threaded everywhere through the heather and bracken, leading from one holt to another or down into the sea. At intervals on each spraints had been deposited, and at the entrances to three large holes were large piles of faeces. We found freshwater pools beside three of the holts and wondered if they had any special significance in the otter way of life. Feeding remains were everywhere – the shells from crab, which by now we were reckoning must form an important part of the diet, and pieces of fish bone and skin. So busy was the whole area that we decided it must be a breeding holt and the cubs old enough to be out and playing. Maybe they were already going down to the shore with their mother. As we turned back for camp we planned to return in the evening to see if there was any action.

There were other islands dotted in the loch which we must visit. They glowed warmly in the midday sun. Seals were basking on their outlying skerries and seemed reluctant to follow the ebbing tide into the sea. To the south we saw a wide estuary and binoculars discovered extensive mud flats backed by coniferous forest. Small rafts of duck were sailing placidly on its shallow waters and oystercatchers were busily probing the mud along the shore. Curlews called plaintively and five herons, nicely spaced out at strategic points, were patiently poised to harpoon their prey. Another place we must surely investigate.

In the afternoon we took the boat over to Eilean Beag – 'the

small island' – and sailed right round it, just to get an idea of what it was like and to find somewhere to land. On the long north side bare rock, sheer, smooth and sombre, fell steeply to the water and narrow ledges threaded along it where sea pinks and other rock plants were growing. There was no access for a boat. As we rounded the eastern end, with its jagged skerry satellites, seals of the common variety slid one by one into the loch where their inquisitive faces with soft sad eyes kept bobbing through the surface to take a look at us. The south side, too, was long, but sloping more gently to the water. On the rock and vegetation above the tideline, gulls were staking out claims to nesting sites. There was plenty of heather, some bracken, and scrub willow growing in sheltered hollows. A few stunted rowans survived fairly exposed conditions and an old pine, struggling for life on the summit, cradled a hooded crow's nest in a fork of its branches. The nest looked as though it might be occupied.

We tied up in a small geo at the west end of the island and scrambled up its sheer sides. Gulls rose in screaming protest and became a restless cloud circling overhead. We hardly noticed them, for at the top, on a boulder covered with moss, was the dark and tarry evidence we were hoping to find – an otter spraint, which must have been deposited there recently, for it was still moist.

This was a good beginning, and we looked around for the best way to set out exploring the island. From beside the boulder a narrow track led off northwards into thick heather in the direction we wanted to follow. We found droppings from red deer, and that could only mean that these animals were swim-ming the considerable distance from the mainland to feed on the heather. Soon we found another spraint, and as we made our way along the northern side of the island another and another. In fact, they appeared so frequently we gave up counting. All the signs of otter presence that we had hoped for were there – in addition to spraints, flattened vegetation where an otter had curled in a circle to sleep, more shell and fish remains on blackened vegetation, and padded down paths that were obviously much in use.

The track we were following continued to the most easterly point of the island where it merged with a cleft in the rock that led down into the sea. In a clump of bracken nearby we nearly

missed a good-sized hole beneath a rock – a secret holt with a small rowan growing beside it. Its entrance was rounded and clear of vegetation, smoothed and impacted by bodies passing through.

It was time to leave the gulls in peace. We had seen enough and suspected that all the islands in the loch would have similar evidence of otters, and later this proved to be the case.

It was while we were walking back along the track that we made a strange discovery. A long rake of rock, smoothed by centuries of pounding waves, sloped down towards the water. It was probably a regular path for otters to and from the loch. At its head was a thick patch of heather, dense and tall. It had hidden from our eyes, on the way in, something that gave us quite a shock. Carefully camouflaged with heather branches and hand-fuls of moss torn from the rocks was a large live-catcher cage. It was set but empty.

'What's going on?' I asked in amazement. This place was meant to be a paradise for otters!

Don shrugged. 'There's no law against trapping and there's still a market for pelts. It makes you sick, though.'

We thought about throwing the whole contraption into the sea, just to show someone our disgust, but he would have others no doubt. In the end we just tripped the catch and scattered the camouflaging material over the adjacent rocks. Whoever it was might get the message.

That evening, before paying another visit to the big holt, we sat quietly in the heather at the top of our rocky outcrop, hoping for sight of an otter passing through the narrows.

'It's a lovely place,' I said. 'Do you think we could manage to come up here fairly regularly?'

'Would be nice to find out more,' Don replied thoughtfully. 'Tents might not be very practical though, and we'd have to find somewhere to leave the boat and outboard. Bringing all the gear each time from home would be an awful nuisance.'

We had fallen in love with both a beautiful and remote area and an elusive and delightful creature. We talked of how a project might be started to study its ways and wondered about a caravan, somewhere on the shores of Loch Dorran, as a permanent base.

Rosy planning was suddenly interrupted by the sound of an

outboard motor from the narrows further north. An evening fisherman? Someone out to enjoy the perfect conditions? Probably – though the trap we had found that afternoon was still in our minds. Perhaps we were children playing cops and robbers but some instinct made us duck out of sight. Was somebody out to check it?

The regular beat of the motor became louder – it was definitely coming our way. Then a small white boat came in sight, chugging steadily through the channel below, and a man with a long thick beard was sitting in the stern. He appeared to be closely watching our shore. Was he looking for us? He would certainly see the tents. We had permission from the owners of the island to camp but we had arrived a day earlier than arranged and had not yet made contact with the warden. If he was the owner of the cage, perhaps he would prefer us not to know about it.

The man sailed on towards the little island, the boat's white paint easy to pick out in the fading light. He seemed in no great hurry, pottering along steadily and perhaps counting the seals on the skerries over there. Then the boat began to creep round behind the island and we heard the engine cut as it glided out of sight. We thought it must be close to the little geo where we had tied up that afternoon.

There was complete silence for a minute. Then, startling against the quiet peace of the evening, all hell was let loose. The gulls. We trained our binoculars on every inch of Eilean Beag that could be covered but saw nothing unusual. Only five minutes passed before we heard the roar of a motor revved, followed by the sound of a steady beat. The man must be away again. The gulls began to settle and very soon the little craft reappeared round the west side of the island, this time making north towards Loch Essan. We sat on for some time but did not hear or see him again.

By now we reckoned it was too late for an otter watch at the big holt – the light would be gone even before we arrived there. Instead we stayed where we were, high above the narrows, admiring a small group of red deer hinds wandering through the birches on the gentle slopes of the mainland opposite and a couple of young stags who joined them. As the mist began to roll in, once more enshrouding all in its evening folds, we found we

could not get the man in the boat out of our minds. It was difficult to know exactly why. He had probably been doing nothing of any consequence, but why had he spent so little time on Eilean Beag and been in such a hurry to leave? We had seen no lobster pots that would need checking.

Early next morning, before packing up, we nipped over to Eilean Beag while no-one was likely to be about. Not greatly to our surprise, the offending trap had been removed.

It was to be some years before otters received the full protection of the law, so at that time there was no reason why someone should not try to catch, or even kill one if they wished. Nevertheless we were uneasy. The trapping of wild animals, in any case, was something we abhorred, but if otters were being taken here on any significant scale it could badly affect the natural balance of their numbers. Maybe whoever it was had found a ready market, either for the live animal or its pelt?

When eventually we returned home, we wrote letters of inquiry to various interested bodies. No very satisfactory replies were received and, in due course, we learned we were no longer welcome to camp on Eilean Mor!

TWO

From Dawn to Dusk

IT WAS SEVERAL YEARS after the momentous visit to Eilean Mor, and my first ever glimpse of an otter, before we finally established a base from which we could get our otter study going. It was surprisingly difficult to find a landowner prepared to believe we would not be a nuisance. Tents were ruled out. We needed something weatherproof and solid in which all our gear and basic foods could be stored, and which would safely house various obstreperous pets that could not be left at home. These have included dogs, cats, a fox cub, a cygnet, and polecats!

Eventually we found a sympathetic estate owner who understood our needs and was willing to give us space. We bought an old caravan, which has done us well, becoming almost an ancient monument. Though it had to be placed in a position less remote than we would have liked, there were certain advantages in having the Estate road just below giving easy access on a long-established track.

We were certainly comfortable. The van was a large one and there was plenty of room for pets, gear and us. The cats, Calum Cat and The Golden Wonder, each had his own 'eyrie', one on a high shelf in a cupboard, the other on top of the dining room sideboard. The dogs, Dirk the gentle German Shepherd and Shian the little collie, had a platform (really the dining area turned upside down) which was their 'place' and on which they thoroughly understood they must remain, at any rate while we were on board. A cage with a run, built underneath, was home to the polecats when we had them.

No-one could have asked for a more beautiful view than we enjoyed from our picture window, a joyful mix of loch, rocky shores, woodland and forest, with long craggy ridges on either side. Behind the caravan, the old woods climbed the steep slope to the open hill and a favourite relaxation after a hard day's work, with the light beginning to go, was to listen to the evening song of wrens, blackbirds, robins, chaffinches and several kinds of warblers, all preparing to roost for the night in the shelter of its trees and understory. It was not uncommon to watch a group of stags or hinds grazing in the field outside and, of course, the local pair of owls spoke to each other, their hooting and kewicking calls often the last sounds heard at the end of the day.

While looking for a base, we had made many visits to Loch Dorran during which we explored the whole expanse of the loch and its environs, discovering otter signs and holts and gaining a general impression of what went on in the otter world there. In due course, as the study progressed, we came to realise that the east end of the loch, stretching from its top to about halfway down its total length, was the part of the range of a dominant dog otter where most of the action took place. His bitches had their breeding holts there and, of course, this was the part of the range where he would be strongly territorial. It seemed, therefore, that if we wanted to learn as much as possible about the otter and its way of life, our best course was to concentrate on this part of the loch rather than to try to cover a much larger area – though we would regularly visit the shores and islands at the western end of the loch to check on the welfare of the otters there.

The physical features of the area could hardly have been better for our purpose. At no part of the range were the shores of Loch Dorran really far apart, especially within the Narrows, so it was possible to pick up and follow otter movement on both sides over the greater part of the loch. We made good use of the rugged rock points which jutted out into the loch and, by each of us going to an agreed position and using radios to keep in touch, were able to observe almost the whole of the inner loch and a large part of the outer. Otter action could also be followed along the shore by stalking the animals. A detailed picture of their way of life was thus built up.

A typical otter watch day would start with the alarm jerking us into consciousness – the time varied, of course, with the seasons. One early October morning it woke me at the reasonably civilised hour of six and I lay warm and comfortable in my sleeping bag, listening fainthearted for the weather outside, half hoping to hear rain lashing at the windows and the wind blowing a gale. That would be useless for otter watching, with animals difficult to discover and action unlikely to be followed up to its natural conclusion. As usual, however, the adrenalin soon began to pump when I took in the stillness of the world outside and thought of a loch without a ripple on its surface. Perfect otter-watching conditions. I glanced at the motionless sleeping bag on the bunk across the passage.

'Are you awake?'

'H'm,' it mumbled before Don began to show any sign of life.

The kettle was put to boil on the battered old stove and, after making sure there were no deer in the field outside, the dogs were let out to stretch their legs and potter about: they would get a longer walk later in the day. We threw on our clothes, packed rucksacks with wet weather clothing and any extras that seemed sensible (cameras, radios and tape recorder) and tidied up. Sleeping bags, clothes, anything edible or chewable, the box under the cooker which acted as trash bin – all proved irresistible to our dogs once they got bored with being left on their own. To the gentle hiss of a cheerful gas heater and beneath the muted light of the old gas lamps, we drank tea and hurried through breakfast. Plans for the day were worked out and agreed.

'If the wind is okay I'll go right down to Eilean Mor and work my way back to Badger Bay,' said Don. 'You go to Rock Point.'

By 'wind' he meant any kind of movement in the air from a full gale to the merest suggestion of a breeze blowing from the wrong direction which would give away our presence to extremely sensitive otter noses.

As we stepped from the van and shut the dogs in firmly behind us the sky to the east glowed warmly with approaching sunrise and inspired the usual magic feelings of anticipation. The faintest breath of a breeze was wafting in from the south west, no more

than one cheek held towards it cool, the other remaining warm. This was good. We would be walking into the wind as we made our way down the loch and would not be likely to disturb any of our otter friends with our scent. Thus we set off on an otter watch which, in the end, turned out to be a special one, for it included a rare event we had never seen before, and perhaps might never see again.

The light was improving as we started across the field towards the wood, the dark waters of the loch turning a shimmering silver grey and its shores, indented with little bays and rugged points all woodland fringed, gradually taking on shape and colour. The bracken rustled softly as we passed, warning the mice of our coming. A willow branch bridge over a burn creaked a gentle protest as we walked on it. The first gull of the day called plaintively from the loch, then floated silently over our heads, observing our presence. Our tawnies kewicked and hooted to each other a final message of the night.

It had been the first cold night of the coming winter and frost crackled beneath our feet as we entered the wood, making it difficult to move quietly. The ancient oaks, mysterious presences from the past, stood silent as we passed but gave up leaves of autumn to fall dead or dying at our feet. Boulders normally mantled in velvet green moss were now decorated in sparkling white – one had a pine marten scat on its top. We scrambled down a narrow track over crisp vegetation to join the Estate road below.

Beside the loch, we looked offshore for the shadowy forms of the boats normally anchored there. The tide lapped lazily at their sides, their bows all pointing south west. Good. Confirmation indeed that the wind would be all right. Turning along the road, and thus into the wind, we surprised six large stags making free of the rich grass lawn of the Big House. Their heads came up sharply to look. One led off, then all were prancing stiff-legged and proud in front of us, fine antlered heads shadowy in the dawn light, their pale, cream-coloured rumps startling against dark winter coats. Up the bank and into the wood they trotted, not too disturbed, for each one at the top paused to look at the intruders below before vanishing out of sight.

The path led on from the lodge, westward through a lovely old

wood of mixed deciduous and coniferous trees, ancient oak and pine, graceful larch, alder and ash, with holly bushes dotted here and there. As we walked slowly and cautiously along, we kept our eyes open for the pair of roe deer often seen there. Suddenly we heard rustling in the dead bracken on the bank to the right. Then a long low shape, dark, with a bushy tail flowing out behind, scurried across the track in front of us and disappeared into a drain on the other side. It was a pine marten and, judging by its size, a male. Coming to the gateway into the field, we found a moist, dark and recently deposited scat in the centre of the track – a marten message for other martens.

As we crossed the big field, the sun rose above the skyline of the loch, lighting a scene which never ceased to delight. To the south, woods of golden-leaved birch and rusty oak lined the rock-bound shore and merged with spruce of deepest green. Dark green forest, patchworked with yellowing larch and dotted with rowan, climbed the steep slopes to reach erratic fingers on to volcanic cliffs. Gloomy gullies, all scree and boulderstrewn, split apart the lowering heights, and ledges, miraculously graced with heather and an occasional rowan sapling, were giant stepping stones to the top. Outcrops of rock, black and forbidding, decorated the long slopes of the ridge above and small groups of sheep and deer were grazing on its rich vegetation.

To the north, on our side of the loch, old woods climbed more gentle slopes to the open hill. The long ridge up there, with its wooded crags, extended all the way to the end of the peninsula and fell in birch-clad slopes to the narrows. Eilean Mor, where we had camped so long ago, was on the other side of the channel. The whole was a landscape of many highland moods, magic in sunshine, menacing in wind and torrential rain, and mysterious in mist that sometimes would not lift all day.

At the far end of the field we climbed the steep track into another old wood and so arrived at the Oakwood Viewpoint. This was a vantage point high above the loch from which most of the Narrows and its shores on the opposite side could be seen. There was the long sweep of Mallard Bay, from Otter Point right up to Birch Point and beyond it, most of the shore down to Seal Island, and Rhuaidh Point below and away to our left. This viewpoint was always known by this name, though there could

have been plenty of others in this wooded place, and it was a regular stopping place for clues to otter presence down below – jaws heard crunching on a fish, young cubs calling for their mothers, or youngsters squabbling and making a great deal of noise about it, or of course the sight of an animal in the water. Today there was nothing, and we were now at the dividing of our ways.

'Okay,' Don said as he shifted his shoulders under the heavy rucksack and yanked it back into position. 'See you later.' He promptly disappeared westwards along a higher path in the wood.

The track down to Rock Point was steep and awkward on this frosty morning, over fallen tree trunks, loose scree and slippery boulders. I walked gingerly and wondered how to arrive at our watching place without making too much noise. The bank was dotted with holly bushes and a robin flitted ahead of me, from one to the other, after a profusion of bright red berries. Pausing beside one of these to admire the colour, a whiff of rotting flesh was suddenly there and could not be ignored. It seemed to come from the shore and might be a dead otter. Better have a look.

I scrambled down a steep bank, the dreadful smell becoming stronger all the while, and close to the loch came quickly to a sorry sight. Here, great chunks of granite, rough-hewn and split apart in another age, lined the shore. Lying between two giant rocks, its hindleg caught in a crack and fractured, was a dead red deer calf. It could not have been there long but already a fox, a hooded crow, even a buzzard or golden eagle, had been busily at work. The poor thing, its faintly spotted coat still beautiful, looked infinitely forlorn. I wondered how long its mother had waited beside it.

I made cautious progress across an area of bog normally so wet it could be tricky, but today doubly treacherous because the frosty night had laid a deceptive crust over all. I crossed a small gully, in summer flaming with yellow iris but now a place of rotting yellowed leaves, and arrived at last at the Rock Point watching place.

This was always an exciting moment. A narrow ledge, which had to be traversed in order to reach the best position, led along one side of the great rock outcrop. Before leaving the shelter of

the wood, the rocks and shore immediately below had to be examined carefully in case of an otter there. Not infrequently the dominant dog of the range would be down there, curled on the seaweed and peacefully sleeping. It seemed to be a favourite place of his. Not only did one not wish to frighten him but it would be extremely aggravating to see him go. It was a small moment of suspense each time – a good start to the day which got the adrenalin going.

Today, after the usual cautious peeking, there was nothing. I shrugged off my rucksack, checked the radio was switched on and its aerial pulled out, told my mini cassette recorder the date, time, state of the tide, wind direction, visibility and my position, then worked along the ledge to my watching place. It was a perfect morning for the purpose, the sun now on the loch and the Narrows so still they were a mirror of reflected seaweed, rock, woodland and craggy heights in which the smallest ripple from a cruising otter would be easily spotted. The shores on each side were glowing in warm, soft light and there were few shadowed places where it would be a problem to pick out an animal. It all looked good.

I settled to a routine checking with binoculars, and a long slow job it was with the tide ebbing to a 'springs' low water and ever-increasing expanses of gleaming brown seaweed to be covered for an animal of more or less identical colour. Particularly difficult were the shallows along the shores, a favourite foraging area, especially for cubs, where floating fronds of seaweed merged imperceptibly with the weed on the shore and restlessly rose and fell with the movement of the water, misleading the observer into thinking an otter there. A small splash from a shallow dive was sometimes the only convincing clue to the animal's presence.

The task was much easier if they were picked up moving over dry rock above the tideline, when dark coats stood out well against the grey of bare granite or the green of surrounding vegetation. There was no lucky break of this sort today, however. I looked in vain for an otter on the shore eating a fish, an otter grooming itself or maybe curled in a hollow sleeping, cubs engaged in an energetic romp, an otter in the water diving, eating, swimming, or perhaps just floating on the tide, its long

body still for once, its tail streaming out behind. For the moment there were none.

After a long stint of not discovering animals that must surely be around somewhere, if only still in their holts, it was tempting to regret not being able to use radio telemetry for the purpose. By this method the otter is fitted with a harness to which is attached a transmitter emitting regular signals that are picked up on headphones from an aerial. The whereabouts of the creature can thus be located. When we started the study, this technique was in its infancy, and in any case we could neither have afforded such equipment nor, as amateurs, were we likely to have been granted a licence to use it. We reckoned we had to learn to recognise the actors in our otter drama by their physical characteristics only.

This was not as difficult as it might seem. Every otter – like all human beings except identical twins – is different. Bodach, the dominant male (often called the Big Dog), was a larger, more powerful animal than the two females, with a broader head and a chunky body. The two females were smaller, more slender of build and easily separated because one had a distinctive pink splodge on her nose and the other an unusually extensive pale chest, throat and chin. They were known as Pinknose and Palethroat respectively. Groupings of cubs were easy for, obligingly, in each season one bitch would have two, the other only one. Sub-adults were more difficult, for as they grew older they often resembled one of their parents and could be mistaken for one of them. Behaviour of any one animal, or a group together, could also provide useful clues as to whom we were watching.

Time passed and still no otters. Instead, to cheer me up, I discovered two stags lying on a patch of seaweed in the little bay to the west of Otter Point. They were contentedly browsing in the first touching there of the autumn sunshine and were beautifully camouflaged, as otters also are, with their background of gleaming browns. I had not seen them arrive, though I ought to have done so, and it was the movement of an antlered head that first caught my attention.

They were young animals, and I was not surprised when a graceful hind stepped down from the wood behind to join them, and then another with a young calf. All had coats that were changing from the tawny of summer to the grey of winter, but

Head of a young male otter – small ears and eyes but profuse and sensitive whiskers which enable it to pick up vibrations from prey underwater

The ideal otter habitat in a Highland seawater loch

The campsite on the island of Eilean Mor
A male sub-adult resting in the weed at water's edge

Sunrise and still water – perfect for otter watching
Pinknose with two well grown cubs in the early morning light

Looking east through
the narrows at Rock
Point

At the caravan –
watching red deer
through the window

the calf's was woollier and softer looking and still had a suggestion of the white spotting it had had at birth. It was a charming family group, unworried by scent or sound of human beings, and so behaving entirely naturally. In a little while, however, the matriarch began to walk delicately over the seaweed back the way she had come. The stags rose from their resting place, somewhat reluctantly I thought, and followed her, and the little calf skipped precariously on the slippery weed to join its mother. Soon they were all climbing on to the rocks of Otter Point to disappear once more into the shelter of the wood.

Then, suddenly, as if magically by the wave of a wizard's wand, there were the otters – three of them foraging in the Narrows between Birch Point and Rhuaidh Point. Where had they come from and how long had they been there? Too often, particularly when the study first started, did we miss these animals actually coming from their holts and entering the loch – it was, after all, but a fleeting business, unless they lingered on the shore.

So who were these three? While they were still in the water it was difficult to see detail, so I started thinking about groupings. We knew that Palethroat had had two cubs that year; that would have meant one otter larger than the other two. But here were two largish otters and only one small. That surely must mean Pinknose with her cub, for she only had one, but who was the third? It certainly was not Bodach, the dominant dog – another possibility – for he was considerably larger than any of the other otters on the range and, in any case, even at that distance, I would have known his face. Oh, well. I would just have to wait and see.

I called Don. 'Do you read me? Over.'

'Sure.'

'I have three otters in the Narrows. Almost certainly Pinknose and cub. Don't know about the other one. They probably came from Birch Point.'

'Ah!' Don replied. 'Palethroat is here in Badger Bay with her two. They came out of the holt in the wood and have been having the usual romp. They're foraging just now.'

At least that was Palethroat sorted out; I now knew exactly where she was. Pinknose, too, soon obliged by giving me an opportunity to confirm that it was indeed her. Rhuaidh Point

was a favourite place for coming ashore and when she caught what looked like a fair-sized eel, it was to this spot that she brought it. Her cub came chasing after her, swimming alongside to try and grab a bite for itself, and when both of them dived, then popped up through the weed and climbed ashore, I recognised both Pinknose's pink splodge and the smaller version which the little one had inherited.

I wanted the third in the group to come ashore too, so that I could positively identify it, but it was still foraging in the centre of the Narrows. Floating with the tide while it ate each catch, it was all the time gradually coming closer to Rock Point, so that soon I should be able to see it better. Then it caught a fish which was large enough to have to bring ashore and swam with it to some rocks not too far away from me. With an effort it dragged the slippery, struggling creature on to the seaweed. Down went its head to tear a mouthful and up it came again, long neck stretched and facing in my direction, to have a good chew. Great! The third pink nose of the morning could be seen clearly through binoculars. This was Pinknose's daughter of last year.

Don called me. 'Palethroat is on the rocks at Marten Point. She brought a lumpsucker to the cubs and is sitting beside them grooming while they eat. How about you?'

I told him.

'I think I'll follow my lot up towards you,' he continued, and I knew he was thinking that the two families might eventually meet – always fun and always interesting.

'Take care of that wind,' I teased – an insult, since Don had long experience of stalking wild animals.

He ignored that one.

'I may stay at Marten Point. It all depends on what she does.'

'Okay.'

By now Pinknose, the small cub and the sub-adult cub were together again, a little group of otters foraging in the Narrows and, without a doubt, approaching closer to Rock Point. Let them please come ashore was my prayer, so that I can get a better look at them – and let Palethroat, if she is coming this way, arrive before they have travelled on elsewhere.

Pinknose caught a large lumpsucker and began to swim as well as she could with the awkward burden towards Rock Point. The

other two at once turned to follow and all three came sailing in to the rocks below me. The mother made her final dive and the other two copied her example. With a considerable effort, hindered by the greedy pair who were trying to grab a bite, she at last dragged the lumpsucker on to the slippery seaweed. Then it was a tearing, chewing, squabbling trio all looking for a bite and making a great deal of noise about it. Hurry up Palethroat, before they finish.

These three were too close for comfort if Don should call me on the radio. I switched off and knew he would understand something interesting was happening. In fact, as Pinknose and company, fish demolished, began to give themselves a good grooming, he crept on all fours along the ledge towards me. I sensed rather than heard him coming and hastily lifted a finger to my lips. He nodded.

'Palethroat and cubs have been over to the Seal Island skerries and are working up towards Otter Point now,' he whispered.

I turned hurriedly to look, and so they were – fast. It looked good for a meeting, though Palethroat could still take it into her head to lead her cubs into a nearby holt. Then she would not come this way at all. We waited anxiously and hoped for the best.

Suddenly everything was happening at once. Palethroat, her family of two faithfully paddling along in line astern, came swimming round the far point of Otter Bay. Immediately Pinknose's head came up and she was scenting with great interest in their direction. As if we needed more excitement, another otter appeared out of the young trees on the top of Otter Point. It was a large one and instantly recognised as Bodach, the dominant dog of the range. As I had seen nothing of him before, I reckoned that he had probably been lying-up in a holt. The Big Dog stood looking in Palethroat's direction, totally engrossed and probably scenting as well as seeing her. As yet, he seemed quite unaware of the other bitch. Surely, in a very few minutes, there would be a great getting-together of otters.

Simultaneously Palethroat and Pinknose whickered, and Bodach, picking up both sounds, whickered loudly too. Pale-throat altered course for the centre of the Narrows and began to swim fast. Her cubs paddled furiously along behind her, trying to keep up. Pinknose and her two, young cub and sub-adult, ran

for the water, fell rather than slipped gracefully in, as they usually did, and began to swim towards Palethroat. Bodach was also hurrying for the water, leaping clumsily from one rock to another, slipping, sliding, tumbling over the wet seaweed.

The big dog otter plunged in and immediately dived into the seaweed world below. The two bitches, with their families, instantly followed him. In no time at all, we had a gloriously obstreperous, energetic, incredibly noisy meeting of otters right in the centre of the Narrows – a wonderful sight!

In the bubbling, splashing, seething cauldron of foaming water it was quite impossible to sort out who was who while they were madly corkscrewing round each other's smooth bodies, swooping into the seaweed forest below, curving and swerving through its restless stems, rising to box and bite, then breaking away to start the game all over again. Excited whickering echoed round the giant rock sides of the Narrows and told the rest of their world that the otters were having a party.

Pinknose suddenly broke away from this whirling maelstrom and began to swim for Otter Point. As if by magic, her own two cubs extricated themselves and obediently followed her example. Then Palethroat seemed to realise what was happening. She whickered gently to her youngsters and they too set off to join the others. Last came an ardent and enthusiastic dominant dog, determined to catch up with them.

They all scrambled ashore as fast as they could, the adults making it on the first attempt, the cubs scrabbling at the weed, slipping and sliding in and out of the water in their hurry. Then the great game continued. Pinknose led away and the rest were immediately after her. It was follow-my-leader, catch-me-if-you-can, pounce, got-you, roll over, kick, break away, and start all over again. It was a great romp, tumbling over the glistening seaweed, sure-footed over bare dry rock, scurrying through the secret heather tunnels at the top of the point, squeaking at the tops of their voices. Seven otters all together at the same moment – a dominant dog, his two bitches, a sub-adult cub and three young ones! Two humble otter watchers nearby almost wept with the joy of it and knew they were never likely to see exactly the same again. Otters are extremely sociable creatures, at least within each family unit, and seem to take advantage of any

opportunity to greet each other, but this had been something special.

The game came to a sudden end. Perhaps they all ran out of steam. Bodach seemed to lose interest, broke away from the party, trotted down the rock on the other side of the point and was last seen swimming across Mallard Bay towards Birch Point. Palethroat set off with her family back towards Seal Island, where we eventually lost sight of them running up a path which we knew led to a holt. Pinknose pottered about on the rocks of Otter Bay for a short while, sniffing them all over, then took her cub into a nearby holt. The young sub-adult had earlier left the group, swimming off round Rock Point and into Marten Bay. In due course, she travelled as far as Badger Bay and was last seen making her way along a path towards a holt.

We sat quietly for a while, each digesting the delightful episode we had just witnessed and keeping an eye open in case, against the odds, there was more otter activity. I was adding to the account on my tape recorder when I noticed Don smiling.

'What is it?' I asked, though I assumed he was still grinning like a Cheshire cat over what we had just seen.

'Look at this,' he said as he drew from his pocket a scruffy old tennis ball. On it were the undeniable marks of otter teeth.

'Where on earth did you find that?' I exclaimed.

'On my way down from Badger Bay I took a quick look at the holt which Palethroat and family must have come from. There were two of them lying beside it!'

'I'll believe anything of otters.' I laughed as I imagined a riotous game, puppy-dog style, in and out of the vegetation. 'But how on earth did they get there?'

It was a fascinating thought. The holt was in a remote place where holidaymakers, if they came at all, would have to walk a very long distance to reach it, or they would have come by boat. In any case, it would have been an odd occasion to be carrying tennis balls around.

The rest of the watch was a bit of an anti-climax, though there is always *something* going on. The remainder of the day included herons, all at their usual stances along the shore and seemingly prepared to wait all day for prey; gulls settling briefly on rocks to preen, or poke and probe the seaweed for titbits; cormorants

diving for fish and sending otter-like ringlets over the water; and a flotilla each of merganser and mallard. But there were no more otters. We waited until the tide had not only turned but had been rising for several hours, and it was just as we were packing up that we saw the last of Bodach. He trundled slowly over the rocks of Birch Point, where he may have been in a holt, slipped into the water and began to swim across Matt's Bay towards the head of the loch. He was still foraging when the light had become too poor to see him.

What a day! Not a typical otter watch, for it had included a new and exciting experience, but that was how it was. Often a watch consisted of patient waiting, checking and checking again for action that never occurred, in spite of what seemed like perfect conditions, the tide ebbing and vast carpets of seaweed on the shore, the loch a millpond in which nothing could be missed. When otters did not appear for long periods, we would start wondering why and regretting the lack of magic infra-red vision, for perhaps these elusive animals had been feeding at night. There were also those tiresome days when the weather was so bad that action in rough water or on sombre rain-lashed seaweed and rock could easily be missed. Then, occasionally, there would be a delightful happening that kept us so totally absorbed that time passed unnoticed.

THREE

Otter Profile

IN PURSUING OUR STUDY it was necessary to make regular and frequent visits to Loch Dorran if a proper record was to be put together, and after the first few years this was achieved when Don retired. There are gaps in the record which could only have been filled by the use of radio telemetry and the wizardry of infra red night vision, but neither of these was available to us. We did, however, have a bonus. The otters Bodach, Pinknose and Pale-throat were easily identified, and were there throughout the most intensive period of our vigil, and well beyond. Gradually, over the months and years, a clear picture of otter behaviour was built up which we believe to be typical and valid. Yet our findings did not always match what we could glean from the available scientific literature.

The otter is a member of the weasel family *Mustelidae*, small to medium sized animals which are remarkable for their long bodies and short legs. They belong to the sub-family *Lutrinae*, and those in Britain are of the species *Lutra lutra*, the Eurasian otter. They vary in size but on average measure something over a metre from nose to tip of tail, the females generally being the smaller. Males weigh around 10kg and females 7kg. It is impossible to assess the otter's lifespan in the wild, but the dominant dog in this story lived to at least ten years old and one of his bitches we knew survived beyond six.

This is an animal that feeds mainly on fish, so it is well adapted to spending much of its life in the water and to the efficient hunting of its prey. The coat is extremely thick and waterproof,

and in conditions that may vary from considerable heat to great cold it keeps the body temperature right. The head is rather flat, offering little resistance to the water, and the feet are webbed. The powerful haunches and a strong rudder-like tail tapering to a point provide the main thrust when travelling fast in water. At such times the forelegs are held close to the chest, but when moving slowly, the animal paddles along rather like a dog. Well-developed claws and strong sharp teeth facilitate the seizing, holding and biting of prey.

On land the otter's senses of hearing and smell are acute but in water both ears and nostrils are closed, so the former is impaired and the latter not available when hunting. In clear water, vision seems to be good, but when it is murky, the animal depends more on sensitive whiskers that pick up vibrations from the movements of its quarry. In bright light on land, its sight appears to be rather poor.

Not so long ago, *Lutra lutra* could be found almost anywhere over a large area stretching from Ireland in the west to Japan in the east, from Arctic Finland in the north to North Africa in the south, as well as in Asia as far south as Indonesia. Within this range there were ten or more sub-species. In recent years, throughout the whole of their range, otter numbers generally have declined, especially from about the middle of this century, and over extensive areas they are now almost, if not altogether absent. The reasons for this are many. Hunting for sport, or for the animal's pelt, certainly played a part, and the animal has been mercilessly put to death by countrymen for its supposed excessive predation on game and fish. Henry Williamson's incomparable and widely read novel *Tarka the Otter* gives us accounts of hunting and persecution which are cruel and which in his time were true to life. The book first appeared in 1927, and it is a sad commentary on the apathy of the general public and of those in authority that for half a century nothing effective was done to protect the otter. In 1975 the otter became a protected species in England and Wales, but it was not until 1981 that the Wildlife and Countryside Act prohibited its killing anywhere in Britain. Ironically, it was the huntsmen who first noticed its decline and though their pursuit of the animal is now illegal, the hunting of mink is not. Does the otter hound know the difference?

By far the most significant cause of the otter's decline is the pollution of its habitat. Industrial waste, including heavy metals and (before they were banned) agricultural pesticides such as dieldrin, have had a devastating effect on the river ecology on which the otter depends for food. The clearing of river banks and other waterways of trees, scrub and vegetation of all kinds denies to the animal proper cover and suitable sites for holts in which to breed. Disturbance from huge numbers of people now using the countryside for recreation could also be significant, in spite of the animal's relative tolerance towards human beings.

Otters still survive in reasonable numbers in Ireland, in parts of Scotland and, to a certain extent, in Wales, Devon and Cornwall. Attempts are also being made to reintroduce them into other areas of the British Isles where once they flourished. In Scotland, where all our otter-watching took place, the animal used not to be found in regions where there was heavy industry or a high density of human population, and numbers in rural areas, where arable or dairy farming was carried on, were greatly reduced. Yet, for reasons not entirely clear, perhaps less pollution, this situation is improving. Otter populations on West Highland coasts, in the Western Isles and in Shetland are healthy and perhaps near the optimum that habitat can support.

It is a common misconception that the otters which live in our estuaries, sea lochs, and along our rocky coastlines are sea otters. This is not the case. *Enhydra lutris* (the sea otter) is a larger animal which belongs to a different species only found on the west coast of North America and along the more remote shores of Japan and North East Asia. It tends to live in large family groups and is relatively tame, so making it easy to hunt for its luxuriant fur. By the beginning of this century it was almost extinct. Nowadays in North America it enjoys the protection of the law, has recovered its numbers relatively quickly, and is now in trouble with abalone fishermen. Another river otter, *Lutra canadensis*, is found in all the Americas and is a different species from our own, though it is similar in its patterns of behaviour.

Our study has been concerned only with the otters whose habitat is the sea loch and rugged coastline of the West Highlands, yet they are river otters (*Lutra lutra*) which survive

happily in either a sea or freshwater environment. It is still a mystery how this animal can eliminate from its system the salt it must inevitably absorb when catching prey in the sea.

As the years went by, our observation of the relationship (or inter-active behaviour) between the dominant male of a range and his bitches and their families appeared to be out of step with the opinions of some other naturalists. We found that contact was made whenever the one became aware of the other in its vicinity, probably by scent on the air or in the water, and usually took the form of excited greetings followed by boisterous but friendly play. It may be that the dominant dog otter which lives in an exclusively freshwater habitat, and whose range may be very extensive, has a quite different relationship with the other otters in his range. Perhaps most of his time, when not hunting, is occupied in discovering where his bitches are when they are in oestrus, and then mating with them. Henry Williamson, who wrote about river otters, portrayed a dog otter who travelled a long way in his rather short life but also managed to have an affectionate relationship with his mates and engaged in play with their families. How much of this behaviour was based on observation and how much was anthropom— not clear.

We found that our coastal otters sel— —t the vicinity of the loch. Day after day they were the— —gh of course we did not —t. Spring, the frog spawning season, which varies with altitude and temperature, was perhaps an exceptional time, when the otters did disappear from the loch. The scene then at nearby freshwater pools and lochans was a devastating one – for the frogs! The otters also tended to vanish when the salmon were entering the rivers to spawn. Coastal otters survive mainly on fish and crustacea and seem only to hunt for rabbits and similar small mammals when they are short of food – or when locally there are large numbers of young inexperienced rabbits available, as is the case in some areas over the summer months. Rabbits are probably caught by digging them out of their burrows. In our area, duck and various ground nesting seabirds are sometimes taken by otters. River habitats or fresh-water lochs may not have fish in the same quantity to prey on, so forcing otters to a greater use of small mammals and wildfowl.

We have never worked with tame or captive otters and therefore have never experienced a human/otter relationship. Our instinct is to avoid unnatural contact because of the risks to the animals. Those that come to trust a human being, so often suffer for it, though clearly this is not always the case. A good deal can be learned about the behaviour and habits of a wild mammal from ones kept in suitable conditions of captivity.

Gavin Maxwell proved as much in his bestselling book *Ring of Bright Water*, written more than thirty years ago, and in others. Of the several species of otter that came into his care, he discovered to a lesser or greater degree that all were capable of trust in human beings, though this trust could not be stretched too far. Accidents did happen. Yet he found his otters affectionate, intelligent, and playful. They also showed long memories when it came to renewing a lapsed relationship. He did not succeed in breeding from his captive otters though Mossy and Monday, who were both Scottish otters, mated and had cubs after they had liberated themselves. They remained within the vicinity of Camusfearna and frequent contact was made with them. More recently Philip Wayre has successfully bred otter cubs from captive animals at his Otter Trust in Norfolk. He found otter bitches so nervous and easily alarmed when giving birth that his are left entirely alone during the process.

Of course it was impossible for us to witness the birth of otter cubs in the wild. In fact the only eye-witness account I have been able to find of otter birth is by the Canadian naturalist Emil Liers. Writing in the American *Journal of Mammalogy* in 1951 of his captive *Lutra canadensis*, he described a delivery lasting 'from 3 to 8 hours, depending in part on the number of young'. His litters varied from two to four cubs whereas I have never seen more than two young in a family at Loch Dorran. 'The mothers that I have watched,' Liers wrote briefly, 'stood on all four feet when bringing forth the cubs. One cub after the other would be dropped until the entire litter was produced.'

Liers is more forthcoming about the nurture of the young in their first few weeks of life:

The female curls tightly around the cubs in such a way that they are almost completely shut off from the cold air. The cubs

are toothless and blind at birth, and are quite helpless for five
or six weeks. The care given the cubs is much the same as that
given by female cats and dogs to their young. The mother licks
them and cleans all feces from the cubs until they are about
seven weeks old ... The eyes open when they are about
thirty-five days old ... and when ten to twelve weeks old the
mother first permits them to exercise and play outside the nest.

In his book *The Private Life of the Otter*, Philip Wayre tells us
that at birth the cubs 'are about 12 cm [less than five inches]
including their tails and are covered with short very pale grey
fur'. He confirms Liers' observation that the cubs are tightly
wrapped in the curled body of the bitch and adds that 'whenever
she moves the cubs chirrup like small birds'.

In 1881 A. H. Cocks FZS published in the 'Proceedings of
the Zoological Society, London' the results of his own experi-
ments in breeding otters, which he considered broke new
ground:

The female was sent to me in March 1873, from North Wales,
as a cub of about 3 lb. weight, with the

until October 1879, when I obtained one in Hamburg. Owing
to the female animal's extreme jealousy, I was not able to let
them run together until they had been duly introduced to each
other through the bars of adjoining cages for some weeks. The
male soon afterwards became very ill with an abscess at the
root of one of his lower pramolar teeth, the result apparently
of some old injury; and although the female occasionally
came in season, he took no notice of her advances, until early
on the morning of July 17th, when they paired in the water,
the female loudly chattering or whistling in a peculiar way
all the while. They remained thus for about an hour; and the
sides of the tank being perpendicular, they were of necessity
swimming the whole time. Nothing further was noticed
until the morning of August 12, when they again paired in
the water. They remained together on this occasion for an
hour and a half (about 6.30 to 8 a.m.).

On October 2, the female being evidently heavy with

young, I separated the animals; and (about 5.45) in the afternoon of the 12th I heard young ones squeaking; in all probability they had not been born more than an hour or two when I discovered them. Reckoning from August 12th (the date of the second pairing), the gestation was therefore 61 days. [A century later Wayre confirmed Cocks's nine to ten and a half weeks as the gestation period.] We constantly heard the cubs squealing; but nothing was seen of them until the 25th, when I looked at them, and found them to be two in number, measuring about 8 inches in length, including the tails, which were about 2 inches, or perhaps rather more, in length, and which were held curved tight round on the abdomen, as in a foetus. They were completely covered with a fine silky coat, very different from the somewhat rough 'puppy-coat' they afterwards assume. They were still blind, with the eyes very prominent. Within two hours after I had looked at them the mother removed them to the other bed-box. From this time they were frequently shifted by the mother from one box to the other, often daily, the longest stay in one box being from October 28th to November 15th.

On November 17, while I was in the act of putting clean straw into the unoccupied bed-box, the Otter came out of the other box with one of the cubs in her mouth, and, swimming with it across the tank, came right up to the box I was filling, as if totally unconscious of my presence. On finding that the bed was not ready, she swam back with the cub across the tank, and although I left the cage as quickly as possible, she made, altogether about six journeys across the tank (which is between 13 and 14 feet long), holding the cub by the neck in her mouth, and carrying it most of the way under water. I could not be sure about its eyes, but believe it to have been still blind. It appeared to be about 15 inches long, or possibly hardly so much. On the 29th the cubs were about 1 foot long in head and body, with tails 6 inches long. Weight probably about 2 lb. Eyes open.

On the night of December 5, one of the cubs first showed itself, lying with its head hanging out of the box. On the 9th the cubs first came out of their own accord, and went into the water several times (both accidentally and purposely it was

supposed); the tank being nearly brimfull, they were able to get out without assistance.

Cocks's reference to a bitch constantly moving her family from one bed-box to another is interesting: we found the breeding holt areas of our wild females to be a complex of holes close to each other, and the same movement may take place between these – for reasons of hygiene, or perhaps because it becomes unpleasantly damp in one or other chamber within.

In the wild at Dorran as the winter months pass, the loch is often gripped in ice, the woods and forests mantled in white and a bitter wind blows. It is then, when we are snugly warm in our sleeping bags, that I will think of our otters Pinknose and Palethroat, and wonder if they are safely in their holts with newly born cubs.

FOUR

Boss Otter

MYSTERIOUS AND EERIE in the half light of dawn, Ben Dorain stood sentinel over the head of the loch. Behind the hill the sky was pale, shot with pink and gold; broad acres of marsh and mud, seaweed and rock, would soon be glowing in the warmth of the rising sun. On the north shore a giant rock, mantled in orange and pale-grey lichen, was sturdily positioned on the oakclad hillside. In a far distant time the ice had brought it there, and now, smoothed and sculpted by the ages and firmly anchored by its own enormous weight, it was the guardian of a secret cavern. Below this monster rock, in its dark dry shelter, the dog otter Bodach had a favourite holt. It marked the eastern boundary of the territory he would defend against any intruding otters on his range.

It was April and we had just returned to Loch Dorran. Yesterday evening, as the light faded, we had seen Bodach, the Big Dog, as we often called him, enter this holt. There had been no hanging about. He had trotted up from the shore and, with no more than a quick sniffing round at the entrance, had vanished below. We imagined a mighty yawn, then a curling at once into a tight ball to sleep. It was too good a chance to miss. If we could catch him leaving in the morning we would follow him down the loch to see what he was up to. For the last four years, sometime during April, both the bitches on the range had brought the new cubs of the season to the shore for the first time. It was always an exciting event, eagerly anticipated. The dog otter's behaviour tomorrow should tell us what we could expect.

With the first glimmerings of dawn, we crept quietly from the car, checked for the direction of the wind, crossed the nearby rough road, and tip-toed up the boulder-strewn slope beside the holt to a position from which we could see its entrance and know that our scent could not reach it. Was our dog still at home? A slight breeze was blowing from the loch over the ebbing tide. Perhaps tantalising scents from the shore would soon persuade him to start his day. If he was there.

Half an hour later a gentle stirring of dead bracken at the hole, a single stalk bending and bouncing back into place, had us tensing for action, and wishing we could see better. A deepening and thickening shadow appeared at the entrance, then a dark shape. Both shadow and shape took on movement. A long low form materialised on the ground in front of the holt. It yawned, scratched and shook itself vigorously. Then, suddenly, it had vanished.

There was a thick clump of reeds in a hollow quite close to the holt, a patch of tall dead heather, thickly branched and dark, and

at each other. Don shrugged. The minutes passed and we began to think of moving to a position from which we could see more of the loch. Then, briefly, fleetingly, an otter stood poised on top of the steep bank that bordered the shore. Silhouetted against reflections of the fiery sky in the loch, the whole animal, large, long and powerful, broad-based tail sweeping out on the ground behind, was undoubtedly Bodach, the dominant dog of the range.

He wasted no time but started down the scree on the other side of the bank, clumsily slipping and sliding over the loose pebbles, then out of control, all four legs locked against disaster, skidded to the bottom. He arrived on the shore, more or less unruffled, shook himself free of the experience, then stood sniffing the air. Moments passed, but there were no alien scents to alarm him. Probably noting again the delicious smell of juicy morsels left behind by the ebbing tide, he trotted briskly down to where the small boulders of the shore became a glistening carpet of seaweed.

The Big Dog hurried busily from one small rock to another

sniffing for something to eat. Huge umbrellas of weed were nosed aside, the fronds parted with an impatient paw. A heaving hump of seaweed was a hungry otter exploring every crack and cranny of the rock beneath. Crab, starfish, eel pout, or any other tasty morsel he could find was seized in his jaws. Head up, the better to chew and swallow, he instantly gobbled them. Often the only clue we had to his whereabouts in the brown weed was the sheen of a long pale throat as he swallowed his victims. Now and again he scented the air and looked carefully round to check for danger. All was well. Hungry after his night in the holt, he placidly continued his search for food.

There was a particularly large rock on the shore which stood out, solitary, against the rest of the weed. It seemed to be an important landmark to the dog. Whenever we had seen him there, and the tide was out, he always visited it. Now, once again, when only a few yards away, he lost interest in feeding and began to trot straight towards it. He seemed to be in a hurry, stumbling on the slippery weed and scrambling clumsily up the barnacle-covered side as fast as he could. He sniffed all over the flat green top of the rock, found its scents satisfactory, carefully positioned himself and, tail up, deposited a spraint – his message for other otters who might visit the rock. Then he scurried down a crevice to the shore.

Beddoch loped towards the water's edge. With no fuss and scarcely a ripple, he slipped in and, with a long curving dive, disappeared. Two hooded crows, disturbed by his passing, flew in on silent wings to squabble over scraps left lying in a hollow. After a tense minute or two, searching the broad sweep of the loch, we reluctantly decided he'd gone for good. This first dive of the animal on entering the water is the beginning of an anxious few moments for the otter-watcher. Will it obligingly pop up again almost at once and be easy to track, or will it travel a considerable distance underwater and, despite attempts to cover every inch of the loch with binoculars, not be found again? You can be sure that once an otter is on a seaweed shore without you seeing it arrive there, it is very difficult to find.

The rugged summit of Ben Dorain was now silhouetted darkly against the radiant backdrop of the sunrise and shadows on the loch were changing from deepest black into softer greys. The

water remained calm. Only the spreading circles of ripples caused by rising fish broke the surface and patterned it with promise for a hungry otter. Bodach must surely be there, somewhere. In the west, the pale, brooding face of the full moon was sinking slowly behind the Eagle Crag. Full moon. The wide expanses of seaweed, which would now be appearing as a result of the spring tides, provided perfect conditions for observing otters. As the minutes passed, we grew impatient for an otter to watch.

'There he is!' Don exclaimed, suddenly.

And so he was, some way out in the loch. We could relax. The Big Dog was floating on his back, eating something from his paws. To him, of course, the scenery was quite irrelevant. The tide was ebbing. There were no alarming scents. He was still hungry and the fish were there. These were the motivation of his movement. He finished his snack, took in a great gulp of air through his mouth, and dived, and seconds later broke surface some hundred yards away with something else to eat. And this was the pattern. Down for some ten to fifteen seconds, then up

otters are foraging, dives will often last anything from seven seconds to sixty, but eleven to twenty-five are the norm. It all depends on the availability of prey.

For the Big Dog, the fishing was good, and knowing the enormous size of otter appetites, we hoped he would stay in the little bay for a while. Eventually he would almost certainly move on down the loch, but if he continued foraging here for a little longer, it would give us a chance to get ahead of him down to Camus Point. We retreated to the car and drove slowly and as quietly as possible along the shore.

Camus Point is a large outcrop of chunky granite topped with heather and grass but with only a stunted rowan or two for otter-watching cover. It was another place the dog otter was almost bound to visit, and only ten minutes later, a small head with a hump behind it and a long tail streaming out over the water, gave him away against the sombre backdrop of Ben Dorain and confirmed our guess. He was close-in to the near shore and floating lazily on the calm waters of Camus Bay.

The dog kept gliding to a halt in the water and paddling gently to keep station. Chin stretched out over the surface, he turned his

head this way and that, as if examining the shore. He was probably scenting, as well. What was he looking for? Of course, if a human being had been there, and too close, he would have vanished at once, but it was more as if he expected to see another otter – friend or foe, we could only guess. Yet, in spite of all this hanging around, the dog was making steady progress along the shore in our direction.

'Better move back a bit,' suggested Don. 'He'll probably come right on to the Point.'

I knew what he meant. Some quirky down-draught might take a whiff of our scent to the otter, and though he seemed often to tolerate our presence quite close, we were taking no chances. A scramble for the water, one little dive, and we would be lucky to see him again.

A string of bubbles mapped Bodach's progress through the shallows. He surfaced just below us and hauled out. He shook himself energetically and a cloud of spray flew into the air and fell as rain on to the rock at his feet. That over, he stood a few moments more, his face towards us, testing the air. We noted, with affection and interest, the broad face, luxuriant whiskers and calm, apparently short-sighted eyes of our dominant dog. We held our breath as he stood there, hesitating. Our scent? We relaxed as he too seemed to relax.

Bodach began to make his way towards the top of the point, leaping from one large boulder to another, not pausing, sure-footed on dry rock. Once there, he proceeded to a large flattened patch of soil close to a clump of bracken. In the centre was a big pile of spraints, some old, dried-up, pale and crumbling, some dark, moist-looking and recently deposited. He sniffed it all over, then evidently pleased with what he had found, added yet another message to the otter world: I have been here; this is my place.

The dog began running and leaping, not very gracefully, back down the route by which he had come. We had a clear view of dark brown head and, in the light of the rising sun, the almost chestnut pelt of back and haunches. He breasted smoothly into the calm waters of the loch, dived and disappeared.

Once again there followed the usual anxious moments. We looked for him foraging. We examined the shore on either side of

the Point. We searched the immediate waters beyond the bays. No sign of the wretch. At last we picked up a small body rising through the water and flipping over in another dive, far out in the centre of the loch and moving fast towards Matt's Bay on the other side. He had what we call a purposeful air about him, as if he had a definite and rather important objective in mind.

We never could find a better way of describing this action. It seemed to happen whenever any of our otters were prompted to move on to something new. What prompted them was not always clear. Sometimes motivation could be directly attributed to their incredible scenting powers, but often it seemed as though a good idea had suddenly occurred and must be immediately acted upon. One of them might be fishing and, suddenly, it was not fishing but swimming fast for another part of the loch. An animal might be eating a fish on the shore when, all at once, discarding its half-finished meal, it would run back into the water and speedily make for somewhere else, often some considerable

to have followed it through binoculars – would the purpose of its journey usually become apparent. It might be to meet another otter. It might be to disappear into a holt or just to start hunting in more productive waters. Whatever the cause, an instant decision had been made and put into effect. It had travelled fast – not pausing to forage – with a purposeful air about it, and would perhaps lead us to an interesting happening in the otter way of life.

The light had improved with the rising of the sun and we were able to follow the Big Dog quite easily, diving, disappearing for long seconds, then popping up again in a fairly predictable position, always markedly further off. In only a few more minutes, after the usual shallow dive that seems almost obligatory when these animals are coming ashore, we picked up a large otter climbing out on to the steep granite ledges of Birch Point. It was, without doubt, the dominant dog.

Birch Point marked the most westerly point of Matt's Bay and was the beginning of the wooded and craggy area which divided it from Mallard Bay. It was a favourite otter place. Birches there were in plenty, but sturdy old oak, a sprinkling of alder and willow, as well. Massive boulders built to a conifer-clad top and

water dripped continuously off the hill to form boggy places where the old tree trunks were perpetually covered in lichen and fallen branches were rotten. Graceful ferns and velvet moss abounded. It was a nice place.

As Bodach reached the top of the steep rocks on the point we had to make a decision. Whenever our otter had finished whatever business he had been engaged in, there were several courses he might follow. He could disappear into a holt. He could return to the water and continue swimming westwards through the Narrows towards the outer loch. Or he could decide to return to the east end and go back into the holt from which he had come; he had, after all, fed well. The problem was that, if his course was through the Narrows, he might travel so fast with the ebbing tide that we would lose him.

'I think I'll wait here,' suggested Don. 'You get down to Rock Point as quick as you can. That should cover most possibilities.'

'Okay. I'll contact you soon.'

This arrangement would mean that the dog otter's action could be monitored continuously. His leisurely examination of the waters and shores around Camus Point, his sniffing over and sprainting on the rocks there, and then his purposeful swim across the loch to a place much visited by the other otters on his range, all suggested he was checking carefully, maybe for intruders. One of his bitches might well be in a holt with cubs.

From the usual watch point in the old oakwood there was nothing to be seen in the Narrows. I ran as quietly as possible over crackling sticks and last year's dead leaves down the rough path that led to Rock Point and slipped, out of breath and too noisily, into our watching place. I thought what a good thing there was only a breath of a breeze and calm water. If Bodach came swimming through the Narrows as fast as he had travelled across the loch, it would be almost impossible to keep track of his progress had it been rough. In fact, he might already be through and have given me the slip.

I got busy checking right away. Mallard Bay appeared to be empty of everything but busily feeding mallard and merganser paddling about in the shallows and merging horribly well with the seaweed; each minor disturbance of the trailing fronds which clothed every small boulder seemed like Bodach nosing about for

titbits. A pair of curlew strutted about importantly, their long bills probing for food. Two oystercatchers, with strident calling, flew fast and low over the loch. The inevitable line-up of patient herons, each earnestly contemplating the waters for prey to harpoon, were spaced out along the shore.

Otter Point, over the way, was devoid of all but a pair of herring gulls perched companionably on a rock, perhaps communing together on where they might nest on Seal Island. One took off, gracefully planing over the shore to another stance; the second followed immediately, alighted close by, then stalked into position by its mate. Languid seals rested tiredly on the rocks of Seal Island and gave me no clues as to otter presence there. The waters of the Narrows seemed devoid of the creatures. Definitely no Bodach.

'I've lost him,' I radio'd to Don in a panic. 'Is he with you?'

'Don't think so,' was his helpful reply. 'Just as you left he ran

dive, and I haven't seen him since.'

'You'd better wait up there, in case he turns up,' I suggested.

'Yes. Okay.'

As I was pushing the radio back into my pocket I heard a lovely crunching sound from the rocks below. Otter jaws at work! How had I missed it? I lay flat on the ledge and slowly, slowly, wriggled forward to peer over. And there it was, head down to the water in a hollow in the seaweed. A pair of hefty haunches was all I could see. It looked big, though, and was eating a large fish. Up came the head, to chew a mouthful and look round thoughtfully. Instant relief. Most certainly, it was Bodach.

It is the easiest thing in the world to miss seeing this well-camouflaged creature whose coat is the colour of the seaweed on the shore, and who, in the water, seems miraculously to take on a grey sheen to match. In a loch glittering in the sunshine, with choppy little waves to confuse the watcher, it is often very difficult to spot and very easy to lose. On the shore, in certain lights, only its movement will give it away. This time, the dog had almost certainly arrived before me – that was my excuse. I should have checked the rocks more carefully. How he had failed

to hear me talking to Don was a mystery. I retreated to a safer position and spoke again.

'It's all right. He's here, right below me. I daren't talk.'

Don's voice was deliberately soft, barely audible. 'Okay. I'll go straight down through the woods to Badger Point in case he goes on down there.'

Another cautious look below and I was just in time to catch the beginning of the next drama. The Big Dog had dropped his fish and was staring, all alert and intensely interested, across the Narrows towards Otter Point. Something there held his attention, and nothing else but another otter would be likely to command such total concentration.

There *was* an otter there! I just caught it scampering down a crevice in the rocks, one which was frequently used by the animals when entering or leaving the water. It was smaller than Bodach, but for the moment I did not recognise it. Bodach whickered excitedly, and made for the water. The two breasted in almost in unison and dived, meeting in the weed on the bottom. A stream of bubbles rose to the surface. The water boiled, erupted as a geyser does, and spewed out two otters clasped together in a writhing, wriggling bundle of ecstatic greetings.

The smaller otter peeled away and began to swim towards Rock Point, Bodach curved round to follow. Both dived, surfaced one after the other, then were paddling in towards the weed. As they clambered out I recognised the unmistakable splodge, the distinctive pink nose of Pinknose. She had been greeting her mate.

Straight away they started another rapturous exchange. It was the bitch who led, flirting with the dog and flaunting her otter charms. He lumbered after her, sometimes getting in a playful nip on her inviting haunches, and each time she squealed and wriggled provocatively away. There was a you-won't-catch-me-but-do-go-on-trying air about her and he, roused, carried on gamely. Perpetual motion. Squeals of excitement. Rough. It was a ritual game played and understood by both.

It came to an end as suddenly as it had started. They broke apart and then, indifferent, as if nothing untoward had been going on, were pottering about on the weed sniffing at this and that. Then, something new on her mind, Pinknose betook herself

to the water, slipped in, dived and was gone. Nonchalantly, as if he too were bored with the proceedings, Bodach returned to the remains of his fish. A couple of mouthfuls was all he wanted. He sniffed the weed where Pinknose had been, dropped a spraint, then followed her into the water. The familiar dive and he had disappeared.

What to do now? Stay put? Dash round into Marten Bay to see if either of them were there? Better find out what was happening with Don.

'Do you read me?'

'Go ahead.'

'Are you at Badger Point, yet?'

'Just got here.'

I told him about Pinknose and Bodach.

He chuckled. 'No wonder he was in such a hurry to leave Birch Point!'

two otters opted for swimming back up through the Narrows, I ought to be able to spot it. Don could cover the outer loch. Only minutes later he was in touch again.

'Bodach's just gone ashore in Marten Bay. He's on the other side of Rock Point, with a fish. No sign of Pinknose.'

'Right. You watch him. I'd better stay here in case she turns up.'

In fact, Pinknose never did. Another half-hour went by during which a great deal of nothing happened and in the end I decided she must have done a typical otter appearing and disappearing act – appearing suddenly from nowhere on Otter Point and then disappearing, just as mysteriously, probably into Mallard Bay. It could have been only a short visit to the loch, for I had not seen her foraging, and when a bitch acts like this, it often indicates a family in the holt that cannot be left for long. By now she was almost certainly back with them.

'There's an otter on Marten Point.' Don sounded excited. 'It's not Palethroat and Bodach is still eating his fish.'

'What about a sub-adult from last season?' I suggested.

'I don't think so. Why don't you go up to the Birch and take a look?'

The Birch is a twisted old tree whose trunk makes a comfort-

able perch to sit on. It is a good place from which to oversee the whole of Marten Bay, the outer waters of Badger Bay and the loch between it and Seal Island. I hurried through the wood sensing something interesting about to happen.

Marten Point is on the far side of the bay when viewed from the Birch. The new otter could be seen clearly there sniffing over the top and, apparently, blissfully unaware of the Big Dog not so far away. Only the merest suggestion of a breeze was drifting on to the shore from the loch so there was no danger of either animal scenting the other. I had a good look through binoculars. Certainly it was neither of the two bitches and rather too big to be a sub-adult. Perhaps it was a young male 'casing the joint' in his search for a vacant territory or a bitch in oestrus.

A curt message from Don. 'Bodach's making a move.'

From my position I could not see him, but very shortly an otter head came into sight in the bay below, two ripples on either side of it spreading out across the still water. It was, of course, the Big Dog. Once again he was making a very leisurely progress, keeping close in to the shore, foraging in the waving fronds of seaweed, floating lazily on the water and looking all around him, as he had before. Was he aware of the newcomer? Unlikely. There was no urgency in his action. Slowly and steadily, he was crossing that bay and, sooner or later, the two otters must become aware of each other and react.

Suddenly, in the shallow water, Bodach rose majestically on to his hind legs, forepaws held folded against his pale chest. He was looking in the direction of Marten Point. Complete attention was followed by instant action. He thumped down into the water, splashing a great shower all around him, and then was swimming fast and furiously for the point. He arrived there with no delay. Then with a shallow dive, a rather clumsy hauling out on to the weed, and a running, leaping, stumbling climb from one rugged boulder to another, he was making for the top as fast as he could.

The strange otter still did not scent the dominant dog. He sat on his haunches, a hind leg busily scratching his chin, and blissfully unaware of approaching retribution. It was sound, not scent, that alerted him. All at once he stopped scratching, scrambled hurriedly and awkwardly on to all fours, glanced

briefly towards the advancing Bodach, and was bolting down the far side of the point for the water. Both vanished from my sight.

About five minutes later Don came back to me on the radio.

'That was great,' he reported, pleased with another piece of otter action to record. 'Bodach really went for him.'

'Was there a scrap?' I wanted to know.

'No. Just the usual seeing-off. Last I saw of the youngster he was swimming hard for the centre of the loch, Eilean Mor way. Bodach gave up quite quickly. He's foraging, now, in Badger Bay.'

It was all just routine to the dominant dog. The intruder, whom we identified as a fairly large male, had been driven out beyond the limits of the territory that Bodach would defend. There is a loosely defined area on the perimeter of each dominant ated. Immature males from the home range seem to operate freely within it for some time, probably until they become competitive for females in oestrus. Then, during the breeding season, both they and any intruders from other ranges are smartly seen off. Aggression rarely takes the form of a serious fight.

Sprainting is of great significance. It is not just a depositing of unwanted matter, the elimination of faeces, but an important means of identification and communication between otters. Each animal has its own scent, which is instantly recognised by the others on a range, and an intruding animal would be discovered quickly. The scent, probably deposited from the anal glands together with the spraint, though relatively mild to the human nose, lingers for a considerable period, weeks rather than days. Sometimes a jelly-like substance is dropped with the spraint, by both the male and the female, and on occasion both will urinate close by. The significance of these acts was never entirely clear to us, but females in oestrus may have been relevant.

All otters are strongly aware each of its own status in the otter world and a seeing-off, or even a spraint message discovered and read correctly, will be sufficient to warn off those who should not be there on the range.

Bodach had just routed an invading male in a manner that animal had instantly understood. The evidence was looking good: the leisurely patrolling along the shores, apparently checking for intruders; the thorough investigation of scent on the points which were regularly visited by the otters on the range; the depositing of his own spraint messages; the ecstatic greetings with Pinknose, but her relatively short visit to the loch – and now, this last action. It would be good to know that Palethroat, too, had motherly responsibilities.

After a short time, the radio called me up.

'The Big Dog has just vanished along the track that leads to a holt,' Don reported. 'He's fed well and will probably stay for a while. I'm going to eat my lunch!'

A good idea. Bodach would probably stay in his holt until the tide had turned and been running for maybe an hour. He might even elect to miss a tide and sleep off a lot of good feeding. Nothing much seemed to be happening at my end. No ducks were feeding in the luxuriant weed, now inert and uninteresting in the slack of the tide. Oystercatchers stood in pairs on the tops of the skerry islets, heads tucked in sleep along gleaming black backs. No curlews called plaintive messages to each other. The seals had deserted Seal Island and were presumably away in island were at peace. All nature rested. The sun was warm. Food might help to keep me awake.

Nearly two hours later, a routine checking of the shores fitted nicely together the last piece of the jigsaw. Near Seal Island, Palethroat – instantly recognised by the extensive patch of pale fur on her chest, chin and cheeks – appeared at the top of a track which led from heather to loch. Without pausing, she ran quickly down the steep ramp to seaweed-covered rock which was rapidly disappearing beneath the incoming tide. For a moment she sniffed around checking the weed for scent, and found nothing of interest. Then she slipped straight into the water and with the usual little flip-over dive disappeared. She popped up in the channel between Rock Point and Seal Island and there began to forage.

'I have Palethroat,' I told Don triumphantly. 'She almost certainly came from one of the holts near Seal Island and is foraging in the middle of the channel towards Rock Point.'

'Good. Bodach's with us again too. He's foraging in Badger Bay.'

I watched Palethroat for nearly half an hour, just steadily diving, eating and diving again. At least she was giving me plenty of views of her chin and cheeks, glinting palely in the sunshine. Positive identification. Somewhere between fifteen and twenty-three seconds was the average length of her dives, and two out of five were successful. She was never far from Seal Island and this staying put in the one location was probably significant. Usually, after a period of foraging in one area, otters set off for another. Palethroat showed no sign of moving on. Had she got cubs?

Then she caught a large lumpsucker and swam ashore with it, her head pulled to one side with the weight of the struggling creature. Instead of dropping her fish on the seaweed and beginning to eat, the bitch struggled back up the ramp from which she had come her prey difficult to control. Twice she dropped it, held it with her paw, then yanked it back into her jaws. At last she arrived at the top, ran straight on along the well-worn track which led to various holts, and vanished. She did not appear again and I imagined a pleasant little otter scene enacted there, with hungry cubs running out to meet her and greedily snatching at the food she had brought. Certainly she would never have bothered to carry that fish to her holt just for her own satisfaction. Cubs she must have and, what was more, they must be old enough to be eating solid food. Quite soon we should be seeing two young families on the shore.

'I have nice news for you,' I started to tell Don.

'Hold it,' he said. 'The Big Dog looks as though he is making for Seal Island. I'm starting back for Rock Point. Keep an eye open in case he goes too fast for me.'

'Okay. Give me ten minutes and I'll move up to Lodge Point.'

From there I would be able to cover the whole length of the Narrows right down to Seal Island while Don was hurrying to his new position. I should pick up Bodach, if he arrived, be able to spot a meeting with Palethroat, if it happened, and see Pinknose, if she came down into the Narrows to forage.

This was rather like planning the moves in an intricate game of chess, but it all became easier, as the years passed and experience was gained. We found, for instance, that the lives of our otters

were very routinely ordered, influenced especially by the movement of the tides. Having discovered one, or a group, it was often
possible to guess correctly what was likely to happen next, and it
was only the exceptional – such as human disturbance or a
sudden change in the weather to rough conditions – that caused
them to disappear or us to lose them.

It was another three hours before we saw the last of Bodach.
He swam over to Seal Island, did a routine checking of the
skerries, fished for a while, and then started an unhurried
inspection of the lochside shore and waters on the south side. It
was really just a repeat performance of the morning, only in the
opposite direction. As we had seen so often, he made use of the
tide, letting it carry him along while he examined the shores and
water for scent, sight or sound of any other otter. When he was
after a fish, though, he turned into the tide to dive, as otters
nearly always seem to do. Once again all the rocky points were
visited, sniffed over and sprainted on.

In due course, Bodach ran down over the granite ledges of
Birch Point to enter Matt's Bay. At the same moment Don
arrived to relieve me at Lodge Point. One of us must now get to
Camus Point as quickly as possible so that we could check
whether the Big Dog returned to the holt from which he had
started his day. The other would remain at Lodge Point from
where it should be possible to check for either of the bitches.
Luckily we had left the car at the limit of the rough road, so for
me it was no more than a quick dash and a drive over the
pot-holed road back to the head of the loch. As I leapt from
the vehicle and crept as quickly as possible into the heather
on Camus Point, the Big Dog came sailing serenely into his
home bay. He foraged there for about ten minutes, had some
luck, then came gliding ashore. He shook himself, trundled
purposefully up the track that led to his holt and, with no more
ado, vanished within. He had had a busy day doing what
dominant dogs have to do, and now the giant lichen-covered
rock would shelter him safely until he felt the urge to move again.

When we met up in the caravan, Don told me he'd seen
nothing more of Pinknose and Palethroat.

Later, as I was writing up the notes for the day, twenty-one
stags came wandering down from the wood to graze peacefully in

the field beside us. Scruffy, they looked, their coats all changing from winter brown to summer red, and in the process of casting their antlers, some still with those of last season, some with only one, others with the stumps from which the new ones would grow. A motley crowd but magnificent all the same. Fascinated by these curious creatures our ginger puss, The Golden Wonder, sat quite still by the window of the caravan, his tail gently twitching.

It had been a good day. Bodach, Pinknose and Palethroat had all given us the clues we were looking for. Beyond reasonable doubt, we would soon see young otter cubs on the shore.

'Did you notice how grey about the muzzle Bodach is becoming?' I asked Don.

'Yes,' he replied thoughtfully. 'I wonder how long otters live

FIVE

Stirrings in the Holt

SPRING FEVER set in each April. The season's new cubs ought soon to be appearing on the shore with their mothers and this would be the start of the most fascinating part of each year's study, interaction between mothers and cubs, families with families, and families with the dominant dog. The daylight hours would be spent in scouring the shores of the loch to catch the golden moment when the bitch mother first led her young to the water. We could never know, of course, whether it actually was

The gestation period, as observed in captive otters, is around sixty-three days. After they are born the young cubs remain in the holt for seven to eight weeks before emerging, and then follow their mother to the shore usually at about ten or eleven, sometimes even earlier. Otter bitches can come into oestrus at any time but on Loch Dorran the cubs are nearly always first seen during the month of April. Working back from that first appearance on the shore, it would seem that mating takes place sometime in the late autumn of the previous year. It is tempting, therefore, to wonder whether the cycle in this area is orientated towards prey species being plentiful when there are hungry youngsters to be fed and the worst of winter gales and rough seas are past before very young cubs are brought to the shore. There are, of course, events which could upset this pattern – the death of the dominant dog and a hiatus when no mating occurs being one – but so far we have been lucky and this has not occurred.

It was now close to the end of April and we had still not found any entrancing young families. All the signs were right. Bodach was regularly patrolling the rocky shores and waters of his territory and – no nonsense about it – had briskly seen off at least two interloping young males. Pinknose, shy and unobtrusive, had seldom been seen out foraging and seemed tied to the part of the loch where she usually bred. Palethroat had not appeared at all. Perhaps she was feeding during the hours of darkness.

We did, now, what we always have to do when this frustrating state of affairs has been reached – crossed the loch to the other side to try to find out what was going on. There are many signs to look for. If there are cubs and they are so young that they are still confined to the holt, we would expect a rather unused appearance to its immediate surroundings. There would be no heavily padded down runways or remnants of food about to give the bitch's presence away, and there would be no piles of spraint, for in this way a minimum of scent is left around. This is really the only defence she has for her cubs against predators – fox, marten, mink, wildcat and stoat – when she has to be away from them.

On the other hand, if we found holes with severely padded down vegetation at their entrances, the whole area looking as though a miniature whirlwind had passed through it, scuffed soil on banks where riotous games had been played, food remains scattered everywhere and growing piles of spraint, we would know for sure that the missing youngsters were old enough now to be soon turning up on the shore – if they had not already done so and we had missed seeing them.

Discovering very young otter cubs on the shore can be quite a problem especially when their much-larger-in-size mother is not present. By sheer luck you may happen upon them, temporarily abandoned while she has gone foraging, and be able to watch their antics for a while. At this stage they have not yet learnt to be wary of human beings. Most of the time you are trying to pick out small brown bodies in an immensity of seaweed that is almost exactly the same colour as they are. Only a small movement, such as a head lifted to look around, or plaintive cries as they call for their parent will give them away.

It was very early in the morning when we set out and the loch

Bodach, the dominant

Pinknose with well grown cub close to shore

Typical otter feeding site with prey remains

Young otter now able to fend for itself

Eel – favourite food. Otter track from shore to holt, often only
6 inches wide, and used also by deer

A cub eating a crab on the weed

Otter holt in a peat bank with spraint at the entrance. Many holts are in rock clefts and some a considerable distance from the loch

was calm, as it so often is in the hour or two around dawn, a mirror waiting to reflect the first happenings of the day. Yet already there was enough light to duplicate the serrated edges of the shore's encompassing crags and the trunks and branches of its woods and forest. They hung motionless in the reflection but shivered gently now and again with tiny movements of the water. Birds making an early start to the day included five gulls chatting amicably together as they passed overhead and five red-throated divers in the centre of the loch sorting out mates for the season with much splashing and chasing and weird haunting cries. The boat lay cradled at our feet in Liath Bay, swinging lazily on the ebbing tide, tapping at welly-booted ankles and insistently reminding us that time was slipping away. We hopped in, shoved off from the shore, then paddled quietly out into deeper water where the outboard could be fired.

A mere drifting in the air from the south west suited our plans. We were off to Birch Point on the other side and would make the final approach on foot from the east end of Matt's Bay. Unless there were otters somewhere completely unexpected and unlikely, they would not be able to scent our coming.

We motored slowly and quietly almost due south and diagon-ally across the loch. Perched in the bows and looking back towards Camus Point, I idly drank in the beauty of the morning, half-dreaming of young otter families on the other side. Then suddenly I blinked. Surely not. But, yes. Backed by the sombre jaggedness of Camus Point and right in the middle of the pale shimmering waters through which we had just sailed was a dark head with paler chin pointed skywards. An otter, energetically chewing on a fish. Only one animal would have tolerated both the sound of the boat and our scent, though much diffused, so close. Bodach!

I signalled hastily to Don and he cut the engine.

'Bodach's in Camus Bay,' I said quietly in the sudden silence.

'What!' It was an exclamation, not a question. He searched and found. 'Well, I'm damned. Where could he have come from?'

The answer to that question one often never knew. Otters seem to suddenly just appear from nowhere. I grabbed my mini-recorder and spoke the first report of the day.

The discovery of the dominant dog turned out to be a bonus.

We sat watching him foraging in the still water, up and down, always diving into the current of the ebbing tide, usually successful, and eating his prey from his paws. To us sitting by, it seemed almost a leisurely process with no great effort involved, but we knew that power pack of energy would be working hard below, streaking through the gloomy depths, swerving, curving, this way and that until he caught his fish. Only the unhurried flip over at the beginning of each dive gave the impression that it was all routine and he had all day in which to satisfy his appetite.

All the time, however, Bodach was gradually moving across the loch towards Matt's Bay and this was cause for alarm. We dared not risk using the motor again, and so were steadily drifting with the tide into the wind and would shortly find ourselves between the shore and the otter. As the length of Matt's Bay slowly but surely passed away and Birch Point loomed nearer, we knew that very soon he must pick up our scent. Then he would promptly disappear.

Just in time, the Big Dog solved the problem for us by catching a large one. We saw him twice lose a struggling monster, dive down after it, and so quickly pop up again with a fish, we assumed it was the same one. The important thing was that the fish was much too big and difficult for him to control and eat in the water, so he would have to take it ashore. Which way would he go? Much to our relief, he set off resolutely for Birch Point, his head held high and to one side to hold the wildly thrashing creature while swimming gamely along. At last he made the final approach dive, paddled the last few feet through the weed and then climbed awkwardly out on to the rock. As he began to eat we recognised the unmistakable red belly of a large lumpsucker and knew that it ought to keep him busy for at least half an hour.

Once we reached the east end of Matt's Bay we cut the engine and used the oars as paddles, finally drifting silently with the tide, and into the wind, to the granite steps of Birch Point. The business of tying up with a long rope to allow, in due course, for a rising tide was routine, and then, since we knew exactly where the Big Dog would probably be, it was simple to follow a deer track to the shore. The unknown was whether or not he had finished his fish and gone, or if other otters were around who might get our scent.

About a third of the way down the promontory lies a pretty little bay backed by a wood of birch. Unimaginatively we call it Little Bay. Sheltered from all winds except those from a northerly direction, and with a shallow safe shore, it is the perfect place for otter mothers to bring their young. Bodach was almost certainly there – we could hear the crunching of fish bones as he munched away on the rocks in that direction – but, as we crept and crawled through the dense dead heather of last season and the sprouting bracken of this, we heard another sound which made us grin at each other with delight. Whickering. One otter does not whicker to itself. There must be two, at least!

'Take it easy,' whispered Don.

'You lead,' I replied, being a coward and afraid of disturbing and losing our quarry.

The final few yards to our watching place took a long time to cover, for each dead twig of winter lay in wait to crack loudly beneath our careless feet and the young bracken rustled and swished as welly boots passed by. It all probably sounded a good deal worse in our ears than it actually was, for when we arrived on the edge of Little Bay, we saw below, on the newly uncovered seaweed, two otters having a boisterous and exceedingly noisy game. One had a beautiful pink splodge on its nose. Pinknose! The other, of course, was her mate, the Big Dog.

Pinknose was being provocative, Bodach was provoked. The bitch was enticing, the dog determined to leap and catch. They slid and stumbled all over the slippery rocks, awkward with their broad, webbed feet, he clumsily ardent, she evasive, elusive, rolling over on to her back to display her charms. Always she squirmed out of reach as he pounced, squeaking and scolding angrily, but each time enticing him to try again. It was as if the bitch was in season, much more a flirtation than just a greeting between two otters who had happened to meet, and might well end in a mating. If it did, then it could only mean that Pinknose did not after all have a family. If that were the case, then a pattern would have been broken and we must find out what was happening.

'No cubs?' whispered Don, both a comment and question in his voice.

'Maybe not,' was the best I could manage.

The energetic game came to a sudden end. Bodach broke away and, ignoring the remains of his fish, lolloped purposefully down to the water's edge. With no backward glance at his lady love, he breasted in, paddled a few yards, then dived.

'You watch him,' I whispered to Don. 'I'll keep an eye on Pinknose.'

Don saw the Big Dog set off westwards into the Narrows and close to the shore. He was in no hurry, often stopping to float lazily on the water while he looked towards the rocks and seaweed that fringed Mallard Bay – typical patrolling action. The gentle breeze was still from the south west so he would be taking on board any interesting scent from those shores. Eventually he ran over the rocks of Otter Point, sprainted, then crossed the Narrows to disappear round the back of Rock Point into Marten Bay.

Pinknose, the opportunist, had polished off the lumpsucker. She gave her coat a meticulous grooming, vigorously scratching and combing it with her sharp, horn-coloured claws. She shook it out, then settled down for a nap. Two herring gulls, standing politely by on a razor edge of rock, hopped down to look for lumpsucker scraps. We were smiling at their pompous strutting, a step or two this way a step the other as sharp eyes searched for winnings, when suddenly the sound we were hoping to hear came ringing loud and clear from the birches to our left. It was the plaintive crying of an otter cub calling for its mother!

Pinknose rose at once, turned to face the wood and whickered a reply. We held our breath. Then from out of the trees, and tumbling down over the old granite rocks, two chubby cubs came running to meet their mother. They looked to be a little more than twelve weeks old and healthy, with dark brown, soft and woolly cub coats.

The family greeted each other in the usual enthusiastic manner of otters, whickering excitedly, winding themselves round and round each other, boxing, biting, pouncing, the cubs all over their mother, leaping on to her back, falling off, trying to catch her tail and nipping into whichever part of her thick coat they could get their teeth.

It all lasted only a few seconds. Pinknose had other plans. She quickly shook them off, whickered a very positive message, and

then made to lead her family over the slippery carpet of weed towards the water. Startled, the cubs stood watching her uncertainly. Surely now was the time for a romp. But their mother whickered again and, used to copying her every action, they scurried to catch her up. What could she be up to, walking on beyond the weed into a very strange world indeed, a shimmering, rippling, frightening place they had never entered before? The youngsters came to a hasty stop: what's this? . . . we're not going in there! Pinknose stood glancing back, waiting for them to follow. They hung back, doubtfully. The scent was somehow right, and it looked like the pool just outside their holt, only much bigger, but there was no reassuring shore on the other side on to which they could leap and, in fact, it did not seem to have another side at all!

The young otters could not know that this terrifying expanse was necessary to their survival and that soon they would be entirely at home in it. Immediately they began a frantic 'peeping'. This sound is not unlike the wistful calling of a meadow pipit, or even a sandpiper, and is sometimes described as a whistle. It is a contact call and quite different from the sharp sound of whickering, which is basically a greeting. Much used between mother and cubs, and cub to cub, the 'peeping' sound carries a long distance and with the movement of the animal's head, as it looks all around it, has a ventriloquistic quality which often makes it difficult to locate. Nevertheless, it can be of great help in finding well-camouflaged youngsters on the seaweed. Other sounds made by otters are chittering, an anger response which can rise almost to a screech, a sort of explosive hiss, '*hah*', which denotes fear when startled, and a companionable chirruping. A warning growl is sometimes heard.

Pinknose ignored her protesting family. Instead she began to paddle slowly about in the quiet waters of the bay, creating a whirlpool of glittering ripples which lapped at the feet of her youngsters and caused them to retreat hastily. Repeatedly she called: come, follow me. Fearful, they huddled on the shore disregarding her commands. Then, at last, encouragement achieving nothing, she swam slowly towards them, shallow-dived and came paddling in.

With a purposeful air the mother climbed the rock beside the

trembling pair. She seized the smaller cub unceremoniously by the scruff and dragged it, submissive now, into the water. The larger cub, perhaps taken by surprise, or instinctively following its sibling, went running in too. Both now panicked and began trying to scramble on to their mother's back, catching her fur in their teeth as she swam, scrabbling with frantic paws at her sides. She rudely rejected them and, whickering reassuringly, began to swim towards the centre of the bay.

The otter mother quite frequently has to take these draconian measures to persuade her cubs into the water. By this time their coats are waterproof and the whole process ought to seem natural enough, since this is the element wherein they will spend a great part of their lives. So often, however, it does not and she has to be quite rough with them. Perhaps it is the sudden transition from an almost dry environment to a totally wet one.

The air was filled with the anxious 'peeping' of the cubs, their small legs working overtime as they paddled furiously to catch their mother. She slowed down a bit, allowing them to come close, but shook them off whenever they tried to climb on to her back. Then, perhaps thinking they had had enough of this new experience for the moment, she wheeled right round to face the shore. In line astern all three returned to shallow water. There Pinknose began a romp, maybe to give them confidence. Fear forgotten in familiar play, the cubs immediately joined in, splashing about in the shallows, spiralling over and under their mother's body, wrapping themselves round and round both her and each other. Mostly their feet made contact with the bottom but often, as they tried to keep up with her, they found themselves dog-paddling along and unconsciously learning to swim. Entangling strands of seaweed caressed their sides and invited them to explore the forest below. Spray flew everywhere and wavelets fanned out to lap greedily at the rocks on the shore.

Only a few seconds later Pinknose broke up the exuberant game. With a vigorous kick of her hindlegs and a flip of her whiplike tail, she took her long lean body streaking into the depths. To the cubs a string of bubbles was all that remained of their vanished mother: what's this ... where's she gone? Immediately frightened, they began 'peeping' and excitedly paddling round and round on the flurried surface. Where was

she? She had disappeared. There was no mother now. The youngsters, soon panicking, made as fast as they could for the shore and safety. They scrambled on to the rocks, turned round to face the loch and began again their plaintive song: we are here . . . where are you? . . . come quickly. Pinknose popped up far out in the centre of the Narrows and, ignoring their cries, began to forage.

'They're not diving yet,' I whispered to Don. 'Do you think this is their first visit to the shore?'

'Difficult to say. They're quite big, but they certainly seem new to it all.'

'What shall we call them?'

'Coll and Cuan, of course.'

These were the names we always gave to each succeeding pair of twin cubs. Both are Gaelic. Coll is the old form meaning a hazel tree and Cuan means the ocean. They sound right in a lovely place where the old names are still used. So far we had never had two sets of twins in the same breeding season to confuse matters, nor had there ever been a litter of three.

When there are two cubs in a family one always seems to be dominant and there is a difference in size which becomes more marked as they grow older. The larger and more aggressive is assumed to be male and the smaller and more timid female; this is usually confirmed at some moment when they are romping on the shore, or grooming, and conveniently displaying their undersides to our inquisitive eyes. Until, as adults, the twins begin each to go its own way, they tend to act always together, playing, foraging, grooming, sleeping, and are seldom far apart. It was convenient for purposes of identifying one family group from the other that each year one bitch had twins, the other a singleton.

The youngsters began a half-hearted rough-and-tumble but it did not last long. Almost at once they were back again on a rock beside the water, calling urgently for their mother. They were hungry and this time she did not keep them waiting. She came swimming in from the Narrows in the customary manner, flipping over, diving, disappearing, breaking the surface again to swim a further distance towards the shore, then diving again. At length she came gliding smoothly across the bay. The cubs saw

her, heard her whicker and began to squeak excitedly. They rushed into the shallows, all fear of the water apparently forgotten, and paddled eagerly to greet her. Food!

The hungry twins homed in on their parent and were soon doing their best to relieve her of a large flapping flounder. To avoid their attentions, and possibly losing the fish, Pinknose shallow-dived down into the weed and became an elusive shape weaving through the seaweed jungle below. Still unable to dive, the cubs comically copied her, paddling along with their heads in the water, anxiously watching the movement of their enticing meal. There was a great churning in the quiet waters of Little Bay and a crescendo of whickering, chittering and chattering, from this boisterous family of otters. The trio came sailing ashore, the bitch still miraculously in control of the fish, the youngsters on either side of her doing their best to grab it. Once on the rocks, Pinknose shook the fish more firmly into place in her jaws, then climbed with difficulty towards a hollow between two seaweed-covered boulders. She dropped the flounder and her unruly family rushed in to squabble and tear at it.

At the same moment two hoodies – dark heads, grey backs, wing pinions spread – floated silently over from the nearby forest, and with a gentle bending of its boughs, alighted on the topmost branches of a birch. From there, with beady speculative eyes, they watched the goings-on below.

Pinknose noted their coming. She was sitting on a rock quite close to her cubs, grooming her coat, but all the time her eyes never left the wicked pair that had just arrived. In fact, just as she was shaking out her clinging wet fur, those boldest of thieving birds came gliding softly down to land only feet away. They began to preen, poking industriously into the feathers on their breasts and backs, pretending no interest whatever in the cubs or the fish. But each time their glossy black heads were raised, twinkling eyes weighed up their chances and step by unassuming step they were sidling closer. Now the otter mother was nonchalantly scratching her chin, eyes never leaving the predatory birds. Her youngsters, completely unaware of the hoodie threat, were squabbling over the flounder.

Suddenly one of the birds darted in with sabre-like bill to seize a morsel. The volcano erupted. Simultaneously, the otter bitch

charged with an angry snarl, the cubs squeaked in alarm, fell away from their fish and went rolling over and over the weed down to the water's edge, and the hoodies rose with harsh scolding cries and a flurry of flapping wings. The bitch crouched, watchful, but made no further move. The young cubs stood uncertainly where they were, bewildered about what to do next. The hoodies, bold birds, strutted forwards again to snatch a scrap. Pinknose was swift. With bristling whiskers and wicked teeth, she hissed, snarled, leapt forwards, and almost caught one of the crows. The thieving pair, with raucous squawks, lifted off and veered away gracefully, indifferently, over the little bay and back to the forest.

The episode over, the bitch toddled down to the water, slipped in without a backward glance at her cubs, and went fishing. Coll and Cuan, the recent stramash forgotten, demolished the remains of their flounder and in a little while, replete and sleepy, curled together for a nap.

It was a pretty scene there in the little bay. Rippling wavelets stroked the shore, retreating further with each languid lapping of the ebbing tide. As its buoyant support receded, the waving fronds of seaweed collapsed in straggling heaps upon the rocks and draped themselves untidily over their sides. The carpet of weed grew ever wider as the tide withdrew, a multi-coloured mantle of brown, orange and yellow tangle pulsating with a hidden life below. Crabs, starfish, eels and all the other creatures harboured within its shelter, scurried for tiny pools and crevices to await its return. The cubs, oblivious to the beauties of nature or the significance of the harvest which might be garnered from beneath the weed, lay comfortably sleeping, one's woolly neck resting softly over the other's. Their mother bobbed up and down in Little Bay, catching herself a meal.

*

'Any sign of Palethroat?' I asked Don, who was trying to watch the loch to the west while I was checking the east.

'Nothing. I think when this lot is over we'd better go down to the other holts and take a look.'

He meant when the action with Pinknose was over, of course, and I agreed. It was strange that we had seen nothing of the

second bitch and were beginning to wonder if anything had happened to her.

Suddenly we heard a sound from far beyond the Narrows which had us cringing. It was a boat, and coming our way – by the sound of it, one with a powerful outboard. This was an unwelcome interruption to which, from time to time, we had to resign ourselves, but usually only in high holiday periods. Quiet fishermen pottering about from one vantage spot to another could be a nuisance, but worse was the unthinking owner of a speedboat or an inflatable. These would come sweeping noisily through the Narrows, creating a great wash that rolled away foaming to the shore. Nothing awful would happen to any otters that were there, except perhaps to very small cubs who could be swept away and drowned. Usually the animals would just disappear, at least for a period if not for good. A natural sequence of events would thus be broken.

'You watch Pinknose,' I whispered, hurriedly. 'I'll keep an eye on the cubs.'

It was all over very quickly. Pinknose, probably aware of the advancing boat long before we were, had dived and next was seen swimming close to her family. She must have whickered for they obeyed an urgent summons and immediately entered the water. The family then completely vanished. That was the only way to describe it. One moment there were cubs splashing in the shallow water, the next there was no sign of them. Just exactly what had happened we had no idea, but they certainly had not run over the shore and back up the path to where their holt would be.

An inflatable boat, with screaming motor and two men shouting to each other, whizzed up the loch, did a great circling round the broad waters of its eastern end, then whizzed down again through the Narrows and out to sea. Soon there was blessed silence once more, with just the gentle lapping of the wash sweeping in. We began looking for our family.

About ten minutes later Pinknose with two small cubs in tow came bravely paddling across the little bay. They must all have been hiding in the seaweed over there, only their noses poking through for life-sustaining air. The family hauled out on to the familiar rocks of their bay and all three shook themselves. A cloud of sparkling spray was rainbowed by the newly risen sun.

We thought that after the recent alarming experience they would either return to their holt or at least have a nap on the shore. Not a bit of it. The mother shook herself again, whickered, then turned to enter the water.

Coll and Cuan followed happily enough, expecting yet another romp in the shallows, but they were, in fact, on the way to yet another new experience. Their mother continued steadily on, paddling through the shallows and out into that frightening world they had only recently entered. Suddenly she vanished, diving deep into the dark waters below, leaving them all alone. She did not reappear, and deserted and hungry once more, the youngsters began to swim agitatedly round and round, searching and calling anxiously.

Pinknose returned almost at once. She had a small eel in her jaws. Ravenous by now, the cubs at once forgot their fear and furiously paddled to meet her, then did their best to grab the fish. What was this? The mother repulsed her eager family, curving away from their snapping teeth, floating in the water and eating the eel herself. Again she flipped over, diving out of their sight. Down into the depths she glided, and caught another small eel but, fending off the desperate Coll and Cuan, she once more ate it herself. The cubs began to 'peep', their plaintive cries echoing across the bay and making us smile so pathetic did they sound: we're hungry . . . feed us.

If she were aware of such things at all, Pinknose would have noted the cries of her young with satisfaction – they were becoming desperate for food and soon would be ready to learn just what she was trying to teach them. She whickered, then dived yet again. This time they got the message. Somewhere down in that mysterious place to which she had vanished were eels. Food. They seemed plentiful and easy to catch. The cubs must follow her down.

It was not as easy as that. There was a problem. They could not get there! The action was hilarious: two small otters doing their best to join their mother in the depths below, heads down, hindlegs desperately kicking, whiplike tails waving round and round like frenzied propellers: kick kick, paddle paddle, thrust thrust; heads up to breathe; heads down again. They did not know it but the air still trapped in their thick woolly coats made

them far too buoyant and quite unable to stay underwater. They kept bobbing back up to the surface like a couple of corks, only to try again and again. At last they were tiring. It was no use. They gave up.

Pinknose came effortlessly swooping up from below and, out of the general confusion which resulted, emerged with a youngster riding on her back. It was Coll, the little male. She dived and this time carried him with her. A bursting of bubbles was the surplus air in his coat rising to the surface and telling us where he was. We imagined the youngster in a weird half-lit world of waving fronds, hanging on to his mother's fur for dear life as she swerved in and out of the tangle, chasing any little fish that were there. In a few moments they came triumphantly sailing up, one after the other because Coll had fallen off, and the bitch allowed him to take a small butterfish from her mouth.

Both cubs, each in turn, rode down into the rich hunting grounds below and because much of the air was worked out of their coats by the water's action soon found they could get there without their mother's help. They discovered an enchanting place where the prey she had always brought them could indeed be found. Hiding in the dim, dark forest of weed, it could be chased, caught and brought to the surface quite easily. Soon they were hunting small items for themselves and demolishing them from their paws, proper otter fashion, on the surface. Another lesson had been learned.

Eventually, perhaps because the youngsters would never at this stage catch enough to satisfy their healthy appetites, Pinknose swam away to the deeper waters of the Narrows where she would probably find bigger prey to hunt. Coll and Cuan instinctively started to follow but again lost their nerve and turned for the shore. They came scuttling back at full speed, scrambled on to the familiar rocks of their little bay and, as ever, began their plaintive song.

They did not have long to wait. Fish were plentiful. We counted the seconds of each dive the bitch made: eleven, seventeen, twenty-three. On the last she was up with another eel, a really large one, and firmly holding the wriggling creature in her jaws, head pulled to one side with the weight of it, she set off slowly but gamely for Little Bay. The fish did its best to shake

itself free but at last Pinknose was safely there. She made the usual shallow dive to come ashore and next was seen emerging, with difficulty, right beside her cubs. They rushed to greet her and grab in their usual boisterous fashion. She pulled the flapping creature securely on to the rocks, dropped it, then left her family to get on with their squabbling.

It was a fine fat meal she had brought, and a fine fierce battle for it that broke out. Coll grabbed the fish, which was still alive and doing its squirming best to escape into the loch, gave it a savage bite on the neck and began to drag it away. Cuan, equally hungry, made an attempt to snatch and got a hold on its tail. There followed a tug-of-war. The young male, aggressive and heavier, tried to pull the fish from his sister to take it to a better position on the rock. She hung on for dear life, grimly determined to get a bite. Coll tore off a sizeable piece and Cuan, without his anchoring weight, dropped the eel and went rolling away over and over on the slippery weed. She skidded to an undignified halt at the water's edge, then raced back again on all fours. The contest was fierce, each cub grimly pulling, giving a little, pulling again, push-me-pull-you, winning a bite, losing the fish for a moment, then grabbing it again. The noise of angry chittering would easily have been heard on the other side of the loch.

At last both cubs could eat no more – it was a very large fish. They began to wander about over the weed in an aimless fashion, sniffing here and there, but really not at all sure what they were wanting to do next. Their mother rose from her resting place on a nearby rock, stretched her long body and yawned. Then she started to roll in the moist seaweed and her cubs, perhaps thinking this the beginning of an excellent game, immediately began to do likewise. Now there were three otters rolling in the weed, one big and two small, legs waving in the air, whipping tails sweeping from side to side, lithe bodies turning and twisting over the cleansing weed, and all of them joyously squeaking with the excitement of it all.

Pinknose rolled right over, began cleaning-up her chin, wiping it along the weed, and again the cubs copied her. In a few moments, that done, she started on her chin, breast, head and stomach, energetically scratching away with the tearing, teasing

claws of her hindleg paws and nibbling away at especially offending places. Finally she gave herself a great shaking. Her gleaming coat fell nicely into place, and as she finished the cubs did their shaking too. All the family were now spruce and clean.

The cubs, of course, had thought this a great game but they were, in fact, learning all about grooming. This is of vital importance to the animals, for otter coats keep their bodies dry when they are in the water and insulate them against considerable variations in temperature both in and out of it. A great deal of time is spent in the exercise. They have a thick undercoat of fairly short hairs, which traps a layer of insulating air and remains dry in the water. The top coat, with longer hairs, is also waterproof and looks all spiky and clinging when the animal first emerges from the water – a good shaking and it falls evenly into place. As with all wild creatures, the youngsters learn the business of survival by copying their mother's example: grooming is one of the lessons. Swimming, diving, catching prey, marking and defending territory are others. All are learned in this fashion, both learning and teaching unconsciously done and entirely instinctive.

'What do you think of them?' I asked Don, risking a word since they were all so busy.

'Super. Between three and four months old, though.'

I seized this opportunity to whisper notes into my mini tape recorder to get it up to the moment. By now we were more than three and a half hours into the action and, when so much is happening, it is all too easy to forget the finer points and the timing.

Soon afterwards something happened which could have frightened the mother into taking her family back into the water and away from Little Bay. A heron (big grey bird with long sharp bill and spindly legs tucked under) came labouring with steady wingbeats over the loch. As it neared one of its favourite fishing stances, those sharpest of bird's eyes spotted us in our hiding place, it raucously announced its displeasure and veered away over the Narrows. Once more we held our breath, fearful of losing the family, but the bitch could neither scent nor see us and to our relief she only lifted her head to watch the bird away.

The heron had not disturbed the otter family but it may have

triggered the mother's next action. She began sniffing carefully over the weed on the nearby rocks. Then, with the usual air of an important mission about to be accomplished, she squatted, raised her tail and deposited a spraint. Both Coll and Cuan did likewise, faithful but comic copiers of their mother's example. She turned away from the loch, began to climb, leap by not-very-graceful leap, to the higher craggy rocks above the shore, then whickered to her children to follow her. She clambered over a few more boulders before glancing back to check on their progress.

No youngsters. They showed no interest in rejoining their mother and were still investigating the scent on the weed and perhaps thinking of starting another romp. The bitch whickered loudly, impatiently, but still the cubs paid no attention. Then she ran back down the rock to her disobedient family and must have said something pretty commanding. At once they turned to follow her. Pinknose, with two scurrying cubs behind, romped away into the shelter of the birches and out of sight along a familiar track. We knew it was the way to one of her holts.

We waited on for another half hour but saw no more of the little family. The whole episode from the moment when we had first seen Bodach, the dominant dog, until Pinknose had vanished into her holt with the cubs had lasted for more than four hours. It was most unlikely that they would reappear soon, for it was now close to low water on a spring tide, a period of slack in which nothing much ever seemed to happen in the otter world. They had all fed well – it was time for sleep in the safety of the holt. There was little chance of Bodach showing up again either until after the tide had turned. We carefully withdrew and walked quietly back to the boat.

The number of breeding bitches on the range of a dominant dog is probably directly related to the availability of prey species. On Loch Dorran the feeding is rich. This abundance, however, is probably also responsible for a fairly high otter population overall in both the inner and outer parts of the loch, and in the adjoining lochs. So the size of each dog's range must be nicely balanced against food supply and the competing requirements of other family units.

Bodach had two bitches and there were two areas in his range which contained their breeding holts. Each was habitually used

by the same bitch each season and it was only during the period when their cubs were confined within the holt that they were at all territorial. Each area was really a complex of holes not too far apart and some, like those of a badger, perhaps connected below ground. One of these would be chosen for the birth. Pinknose and her family were now safely in their holt, or maybe curled in the bracken close-by, having a nap. We still had to solve the problem of Palethroat. Where was she and what was she doing?

Before crossing the loch back to base, we paddled and drifted with the last of the tide down through the Narrows to the other holt complex but found no sign at all that any of its holes was in use. A further three hours watching from the opposite side of the loch revealed no sign of the missing bitch. Bodach we did see, however, swimming lazily across the waters of Badger Bay and giving every appearance of having begun his patrolling duties once again. He would make his way back up the loch on the rising tide. It had been a busy day.

SIX

A Pinknose and a Palethroat

IT WAS CLOSE to the end of May. Pinknose and cubs were doing well, Bodach was behaving as he should, but we had failed as yet to find Palethroat, with or without a family. Nearly four weeks had passed since we had examined the holt area where she, so far, had always had her cubs, and saw no sign of any activity. That, in itself, did not greatly concern us – perhaps, at last, the customary pattern of breeding had been broken and she had not been mated at the usual time. It was more that we had been keeping a sharp look-out for her both from Badger Point and Rock Point, points from which all the parts of the loch where she would feed were visible, but no Palethroat bitch had been discovered. Why?

Of course there was always the lobster creel. Death by drowning in one of these was a distinct possibility in this area, but so far as we knew it happened but rarely. There were few hazards to cause other than natural death to otters: no roads suitable for fast traffic, one of the most common causes of otter deaths; no trapping or shooting so far as we knew, the animal now being protected by law. So it seemed most unlikely that anything drastic had happened to Palethroat, but if that comparatively young animal was dead, we wanted to know what had happened.

That was the situation when, early one morning at five o'clock, I slipped quietly into my usual watching place at Rock Point. Don was on his way to Badger Point. There was promise of sunrise in a glowing golden sky to the east and a slight haze over

the loch which should mean a warm day to follow. No wind at all ruffled the water, so no creature on its glass-like surface could possibly be missed. An early hatch of midges foretold those voracious hordes which in the coming weeks would make our lives a misery. No amount of midge repellant stands up to several minutes, let alone hours, of total immobility on the part of the victim and veils, though effective, do mean reduced visibility.

The utter stillness was broken only by two cormorants fishing in the Narrows, the quiet plops of their diving kidding me each time into thinking an otter must be somewhere around. Otter Point opposite was shedding its mantle of early morning mist and, as ever, prompting thoughts of a stage perfectly set for a drama of otters. A mallard duck with nine little ducklings in a neatly ordered line behind her paddled bravely through the Narrows and continued on towards the dimly seen rocks of Rhuaidh Point. I thought of the hazards that beset these little gems and wondered what the count would be in a week or two. A family of ravens practised intricate manoeuvres in the sky above, both parents and fledglings soaring heavenwards, swooping to tangle with each other, tumbling earthwards, and then starting all over again. All the time they chatted companionably together – '*cruk, cruk, cruk*' – deeper sound from adults, higher pitched from the young.

The gulls on Seal Island, nesting space booked, were all sitting on eggs. There were charming ceremonies of greeting, as one parent relieved the other on the nest, a standing close together, a bowing to each other and sometimes a noisy mating. Beneath them, on the rocks below, common seal mothers were staking out claims to breeding space. There seemed to be a great many of them this year, and I wondered how this would affect the behaviour of our otters. In a week or two the air would be filled with the mournful calling of seal pups, and their mothers, normally tolerant of otter activity, would become extremely protective. The animal we were trying to watch would become elusive and difficult to find, hugging the shoreline, skulking in the shallows within the shelter of the weed and avoiding its large neighbours wherever possible.

A ponderous male seal, darkest grey with bite marks in the region of his neck, porpoised along through the Narrows,

snorting, blowing, and slapping himself down in the water with resounding smacks. He came gliding in towards the skerries of Rock Point, immediately below me, and sad eyes examined each weed-encrusted rock. Mating time was a long way off yet, but perhaps he checked over his territory when pups were about to be born. He planed smoothly past my watching place, then sank without a sound into darker, deeper waters.

My radio crackled. I whipped it out of my pocket, sure there would be exciting happenings on this perfect morning. As Don spoke I automatically reached for the tape recorder.

'Good morning!' An irrelevance with which he always started the day. 'Good news. There's a cub here in Badger Bay!'

He sounded pleased, as if he himself had been personally responsible for conjuring it up, and I knew the clipped message meant something like: this must surely be Palethroat's cub, at last.

'Great,' I replied, cautiously. 'How big is it?'

'Well, certainly bigger than Pinknose's, perhaps six months old, and it looks like a male.'

'What is it doing?'

'Just paddling about in the shallows below me, peeping. He's a nice little chap. Listen a minute.'

On my radio I picked up the plaintive urgent calling of a cub as it swam about in the water, fading away to nothing, then moving closer again until it was quite loud.

'With all that racket, the mother should come soon,' I laughed. 'Then we'll know for sure whose it is!'

'Don't you believe it's Palethroat's?' He sounded reproachful.

'Of course it's hers!'

The day had started well. It was always a pleasant moment when the first action occurred, but this news was particularly satisfactory. Perhaps the mystery of Palethroat was about to be unfolded and part of the fun would be in making sure that this was indeed her cub. Suppose there was a new bitch, with a cub, on the range? Maybe one of the sub-adult females had been mated? Both seemed unlikely in view of her comparative youth, but we would need to make sure. I checked the time and repeated the information Don had given me into the recorder and wished I could be up at Badger Bay where it was all likely to happen.

No otters, as yet, to be seen at my end of the loch, only one, two, three lone seals all making a leisurely progress down through the Narrows. With each regular sinking into the depths, they created ripples on the water that needed a second look from me, just to make sure they were not those made by otters.

A few minutes later Don was back on the radio. He sounded quite excited.

'Are you there?'

'Of course.'

'There's an otter swimming over from Seal Island. Looks as though it is coming my way. It's big!'

'Bet you think it's Palethroat,' I teased.

He laughed. 'Of course. Keep listening.'

From Rock Point another routine checking of the Narrows and inner loch. Still no otters. The cormorants had moved up the loch and were fishing now off Birch Point where glossy crested heads shone greenly black in the risen sun. The raven family had settled on the grassy ridge above the Narrows, the parents each on a boulder preening feathers of deepest black, the young strutting importantly about poking at this and that with their bills. The mallard duck had led her youngsters into the shallow waters of Mallard Bay, dainty brown balls of fluff bobbing up and down in flowing strands of seaweed.

About five minutes later the radio came to life. 'That otter is coming into the bay. It has a large fish. It's not Palethroat. It's the Dog!'

Don sounded surprised, curious, even disconcerted, as though he felt he ought to have recognised his old friend Bodach before now. I could not think why – a large otter carrying a fish would be almost impossible to identify at a distance.

'So?' I asked, wondering what all the excitement was about. A pity it was not Palethroat, but really there was no special reason why the dog otter should not be bringing a large fish ashore to eat – he just happened to be bringing it into Badger Bay.

'Just you wait,' he said. 'This is going to be interesting.'

He was right. The following are the staccato sentences which came to me over the radio, without any comment from me since I was far too busy repeating them all into the recorder.

'The cub is still swimming up and down along the shore and

calling loudly ... it must be very hungry ... perhaps something's happened to its mother ... Bodach is swimming into
Badger Bay ... he's still got the fish on board ... he's making
straight for the cub ... he's dived ... he's up again ... he's
whickered and the cub is dashing to meet him, is trying to grab
the fish ... they're both swimming for the rock below me ...
they're bound to see me ... the cub's hanging on to the fish ...
they're coming ashore ... Bodach's dragging the fish, it's a
lumpsucker, higher on to the rock ... good lord, he's actually
dropped it right in front of the cub and the cub is eating ... the
dog is on a rock, quite close, grooming ... now he's showing
interest in the fish, trying to get a bite ... you'll not believe this,
the cub is pulling the fish away, cheeky blighter!'

'What do you make of all that?' Don asked a few moments
later when finally he could catch his breath.

It certainly had been a fascinating episode. It appeared that the
dog had brought the fish specifically for the cub and not for
himself. Had he heard it calling and responded? The cub had
greeted him in exactly the same manner as he would have greeted
his mother, accepting the fish and seeming to take his male parent
entirely for granted. Was this something that happened quite
frequently? We thought not too often. Right at the start of the
study we had read that the dominant dog of a range had no part to
play in the rearing of his cubs. His function was to father them
and to guard his territory. But we had not found this to be the
case. Whenever he came across one of his families in his patrolling activity, there were always rapturous, though usually brief,
greetings. This was the first time we had seen him actually feed a
cub.

'Are you absolutely sure it's Bodach?' I teased.

'Of course I'm sure. I can see both of them perfectly, and why
they haven't heard me talking to you I can't think.'

While I was feeding all this into the tape recorder, I suddenly
noticed my mallard lady, now swimming diligently with her
family over Mallard Bay, suddenly swerve off course as if to
avoid an obstacle floating in the water. Her chicks, in strict
formation behind her, and as if ordered by a regimental sergeant
major, halted as one, did a sharp left turn followed shortly by a
turn right, then paddled on serenely once more neatly in line

astern. A v-shaped ripple, broken apart then coming together again, appeared from out of the original course the mallards had been following. An otter was crossing their path, and it had two small cubs hurrying along behind. Unless we had a stranger on the loch also with a pair of cubs, it had to be Pinknose.

I watched the otter mother coming closer and closer to Rhuaidh Point, a favourite place to which she often brought her cubs, and radio'd Don.

'Pinknose and family have just crossed over from Birch Point and are coming ashore on Rhuaidh Point. At least, it's almost certainly her – I can't see her nose yet! What's happening with you?'

'I was just going to get in touch. Bodach is back in the water and is foraging across Badger Bay towards Marten Point. The cub has gone to sleep on a rock below me. Anything special about Pinknose, if it is her?'

'Not really. The cubs seem happy enough now to follow her right over the loch. They're swimming strongly.'

'Okay. We'll be in touch.'

Pinknose and family did indeed come ashore on Rhuaidh Point, but only for a brief visit – just time enough to confirm the untidy pink patch on the bitch's nose. There was the usual carry-on, all of them shaking out the water from their coats and doing a spot of scratching, but after a very short break the mother entered the water again and the cubs followed her example.

They all began to forage, and it was so shallow that Pinknose just stood on all fours, head down nosing into the water, and lifting whatever she caught into the air to eat. The cubs' legs were not long enough for this easy method, so with heads down and necks stretched to the limit, they were kicking hard into the weed and not having much success in catching whatever was down there. Even from Rock Point it was amusing to watch their antics, and had I not already known there was a little group of otters there, the flurry in the water, the bouncing, bubbling, foaming agitation, would have led me to them right away.

The cubs, who of course were Coll and Cuan, had made great progress since that day several weeks ago when we had seen their mother dragging them into the water and teaching them to hunt. At the moment, though, they were hungry and only catching

titbits. Pinknose began to move further out into the Narrows, into deeper, more productive waters. Once again there was no problem with her family, which followed confidently, happy to leave the shore. Soon all three were popping up and down, busily fishing away and catching bigger prey. It became quite tricky keeping tabs on them all: two down, one up; three up; three down; one down, two up; and so on. As to what they were all eating it was impossible to see.

All the while this little group was slowly but steadily making its way down the loch towards Rock Point. It looked as though they might come on to the rocks below me, and if that happened, it would be impossible to talk with Don. I had better get in touch before it was too late.

'Are you there?'

'Yes, but I can only whisper,' he replied at once. 'Guess who has arrived?'

'Not Palethroat!'

'Yes, only minutes ago. She and the cub are having a terrific romp just below me.'

'You're sure it's her?' I asked, finding it difficult to believe we had at last found the second bitch.

'Come on!' was my husband's reproachful retort.

'Where do you think she's been all this time?'

'Goodness knows. We'll talk about it later. I had just been going to contact you. Bodach has swum over to Seal Island, so watch out for him. How about Pinknose?'

I told him what had been happening and we agreed to switch off for half an hour since we both might have otters too close for comfort. They do, after all, have extremely good hearing. Don would then get in touch with me if he could do so without disturbing any action.

There followed half an hour or so of watching Pinknose and family, obviously hungry and the fishing good. Otter Point, across the way, was now completely clear of mist and as always, with its memories of so many otter occasions, it cast a spell. The seaweed-embroidered rocks at its base, the giant boulders split apart by millions of years of battering by stormy seas, its verdant top of luscious grasses backed by a small wood of conifer and birch, all presented an inviting stage upon which I was sure an

otter drama must soon take place. I still hoped, of course, that Pinknose and company would come ashore just below me because there is no thrill better than being only feet away from any wild animal so that you can almost feel the soft thickness of its fur and can certainly smell the rich aroma of its body.

While I was also keeping an eye open for Bodach, over at Seal Island or in the water beyond Rock Point, I found myself working on the problem of Palethroat. It was good that she had been discovered at last, but what had she been doing and where had she been? Why had we not seen her on the shore with her cub at about the same time as the others? Or before that, if her cub was older, as Don had suggested.

Then I remembered the yacht. Easter had fallen at the beginning of April and there had been holiday people about. One morning we had been at our usual watching places, early as ever, and had noted a large yacht setting sail out of Seal Island Bay for the outer loch and the sea. It was most unlikely, at that time of the day, that it had just arrived, turned around and was leaving again at once. In all probability it had sailed in late the evening before and had anchored in the bay for the night. The crew would have gone ashore to stretch their legs, would probably have taken dogs as well, perhaps terriers which would be quite capable of penetrating into the holt of an otter. My heated imagination also convinced me that the intruders had had a barbecue as well and a noisy party long into the night.

These good people probably congratulated themselves on finding a nice secluded place in which to anchor and were not to know that close by in a holt an otter bitch had her family. That family, in this case, would have been old enough to be playing around the holt or even visiting the shore. The mother may have panicked and decided to take her cub elsewhere. Slipping silently round the other side of the rock, the little one instinctively quiet, the yacht people quite unaware, she may have swum with it on her back to the other side of the loch. Over there, near the limit of the range, were several holts to which she might go. Added to all this, I decided Palethroat had been foraging and bringing her cub to the shore only at night. Otherwise, how could we have failed to see her?

Nice neat explanations and probably far from the truth.

Almost certainly we would never know why she had not reared her cub in the usual breeding place. Perhaps she had never even been there.

Bodach interrupted my fantasising. Checking routinely towards Seal Island and the outer loch, I suddenly picked up an otter foraging close to the skerry rocks. The distance is small from Rock Point and I was soon able to confirm it was the dominant dog. Good. He was probably making his way gradually back up the loch but was certainly in no hurry, finding plenty to catch and eat on the way. I wondered if he would meet up with Pinknose and her family, or whether chance would take him into a holt before that could happen, where he would rest until the tide had turned.

Don, as we had arranged, should have called me by now. He had not. It would have been good to know what was going on with him and to get him up to date on my lot. Maybe he had action too close.

Bodach certainly seemed to be doing his territorial checking act as well as finding food for himself. Every so often he scrambled out on to a prominent rock to sniff it over thoroughly and deposit a spraint. Back in the water, he paddled gently to keep station while his calm eyes glanced all around for intruders. Now and again he rose high in the water to scent the gentle breeze.

There was a small interlude when he had a problem with four female seals. On a length of rock, one to which Bodach wished to bring a fish he had caught, they lay spaced out on comfortable beds of seaweed, languid, lazy, and hugely pregnant in the warmth of the midday sun. They looked profoundly uncomfortable to the human eye but were evidently happy enough dozing in the sunshine and not in the least interested in what might be going on about them. At least, that was how it seemed until the dominant dog came along, paddling purposefully in with his prey in his mouth. The nearest torpid seal came instantly to life. Her head turned slowly in his direction and a speculative eye was cast on this invader of her territory. Undoubtedly a message of some importance was passed, for the otter needed no further prompting. He came abruptly to a halt and, turning awkwardly in his tracks in the shallow water, swerved away and swam off

discomfited. Not too abashed, he tried three more likely places on the rock and found three more seals awaiting him. Each told him to 'push off' in a manner he thoroughly understood, so he gave up, dived with his fish, and safely landed it on a different skerry altogether.

Normally there is no agro between common seals and otters, each ignoring the other most of the time, even making use of the same rocks to haul out on and doing their hunting in the same parts of the loch. In the breeding season, however, when both may have young, otters are respectful of their larger neighbours which do not like them too near their pups, and they become secretive and difficult to see, making much use of the cover of seaweed and taking avoiding action if they find a seal too close on the rocks. At these times otters probably do most of their feeding at night, to avoid the diurnal seals.

I tried calling Don, but there was still no reply. He must have exciting action to watch down there. Maddening! I wanted to know what was happening.

Meantime Pinknose and family were working gradually over the Narrows towards Otter Point and the Big Dog was now foraging in one of the little bays to the west of that point. The drift of air was still from the south west and at some moment the bitch would pick up the dog otter's scent, and with the tide still ebbing, he might well discover her scent strong on the water. There was surely going to be a meeting.

It all happened rather quickly. Pinknose was suddenly swimming fast for Otter Point and Coll and Cuan were scurrying to catch up with her. Bodach was on his way across Otter Bay. Pinknose dived, the cubs dived, then all three were hauling out on to the lower rocks of the point. There was a shower of shaken out droplets. Then they were standing, ears pricked and noses pointing, staring fixedly into the Narrows. Bodach too had come to a halt. He rose high out of the water, pale throat glinting in the sunlight, and was scenting with great interest towards Otter Point.

Both otters whickered. Pinknose plunged back into the water and her family followed. She tore off towards the dog and he to her – both on collision course. The adults dived, the cubs dived, and there was a great boiling and bubbling of the waters in the

middle of the Narrows as they met in the seaweed forest below. They all rose triumphantly and noisily out of the depths, a turmoil of jubilant otters, and began swimming for the point. Almost immediately they were hurrying ashore.

There was much whickering as they hauled out on to the rock, two large and two small otters all telling each other how nice it was to meet. Pinknose led away over the slippery seaweed, clumsily leaping over crevices between rocks, stumbling from one boulder to another, and egging them on to a game. Bodach, taking on the challenge and eager to catch, started after her, and Coll and Cuan, nipping each other in their excitement and nipping their father too, scurried after to join in the fun. Once on the smooth, bare lichen-encrusted rocks near the top, they were into the usual tumultuous game, boxing, biting, rolling over and over, squirming away, leaping, pouncing, running away into the trees, running back out again to surprise from another place, a rumbustious romping of otters which we never tired of watching. As usual, the noise they made, the whickering, squeaking, growling, snarling, resounded all round the loch and gave away their presence.

As usual, too, it was quickly over. Bodach, the steam gone out of him, broke away and began nonchalantly wandering over the rock, sniffing it over thoroughly and sprainting twice. The bitch and the cubs left him respectfully alone. He entered the water on the Mallard Bay side and began to forage across the bay towards Birch Point. Pinknose and family sat themselves down and started diligently cleaning up their ruffled fur coats. They seemed happily set to be there for a while.

It was time to try and contact Don again, to see what was happening with him. As I was pulling my radio from my pocket, there was a quiet rustling in the wood behind me and next moment, with a grin and his finger to his lips, the man himself was cautiously creeping over the ledge towards me.

'Sorry about the radio.' He spoke before I could get in a protest. 'I'll tell you all about it later. The important thing is that Palethroat and cub are now in Marten Bay. I followed them along. What's happening here?'

It might be thought surprising that Don had joined me at Rock Point. How could he properly watch whatever might be going on

in the outer loch from there? Well, he already knew from me that Pinknose and family were somewhere in the Narrows, and when he saw Palethroat enter Marten Bay, almost certainly on her way up the loch, he felt there was a good chance of the two families meeting. He had also made sure that Bodach had not done the unlikely thing and returned to Badger Bay. So all the action was likely now to be in the Narrows, or perhaps at Seal Island. In the event of Palethroat suddenly deciding to make her way back to Badger Bay, he would easily spot her doing so from our watch-point and then follow her down there. If she stayed too long in Marten Bay, he could easily nip round to see what she was up to.

If there was to be action, however, we felt sure it would come soon. It was close on midday, and already there was that indefinable something in the air – that feeling we always noticed in summertime – when nature was about to have a siesta hour, when all creatures rested and nothing much was likely to happen. When this time also coincided with low water – not far off now, though on a neap tide so there would still be plenty of water in the Narrows – otters did not seem to do much in the way of foraging, and rested too. By this stage of the study we had seen plenty of meetings between the two bitches and their respective cubs, but there was always the chance of something new happening and the occasions never lost their charm. Pinknose and Palethroat had better hurry up!

Bodach evidently thought it was siesta time. He had worked across Mallard Bay in a leisurely sort of way, foraging and doing his patrolling act as well, when suddenly I saw him swimming purposefully for the rocks of Birch Point. He hauled out, shook himself thoroughly, sprainted, then ran straight over the weed and up a large cleft in the rock. He did not reappear and was probably in a holt.

Pinknose and her cubs were also resting, comfortably curled together in a bundle on Otter Point. Only the bitch's head was regularly raised in order to look around and scent. We wondered if they would just stay put there until the tide had turned and once again there was movement in the water. And what was Palethroat doing? Had she also decided it was time for a break and curled with her cub on one of her favourite rocks in Marten Bay? In a minute one of us would go and see.

Palethroat's cub would be called Caorunn. That was the name we always gave to a singleton cub regardless of its sex and, so far, both bitches had not each produced two in a season. While I added him into the notes and got them up to the minute, Don kept an eye on the loch. It was all rather sleepy and relaxed. Maybe we, too, should have a siesta . . .

Palethroat was not asleep. Suddenly she came sailing serenely round the base of Rock Point, a v-shaped ripple containing the smaller 'v' of her cub, fanning out over the sluggish waters on either side. She glanced briefly up at the bare sheer sides of the point, evidently saw or scented nothing of interest, and continued swimming on into the Narrows. Then she whickered. The sound rang out clear and decisive, over the Narrows: I'm here; you're there; let's meet.

Pinknose and the cubs sprang into instant life. For a moment all three stood startled on the rock, staring, scenting, listening. Then the call came again and immediately they were running, stumbling, sliding to the water. With no hesitation at all they tore in and began swimming towards the other bitch. Pinknose whickered. Palethroat replied. Then both, simultaneously and faithfully followed by their cubs, dived into the deeper water in the centre of the Narrows, and disappeared.

For a long moment nothing happened and all we could see was disturbed water full of particles of sand and silt. Then, somewhere in the tangle forest below, there was an eruption of boiling, bubbling water. It was a meeting of two otter families. All five shot through the surface and, whiskers glinting in the sunshine, rose high in the water to greet each other. It was a great boxing and biting, diving and chasing, corkscrewing over and under, of exuberant otters all whickering at the tops of their voices.

The proceedings, as always, came to a sudden end – it was as though they all switched off at the same moment – and this was when things became really interesting. Palethroat, evidently happy to leave her quite large cub to fend for itself, swam round into Mallard Bay and began to forage. Pinknose, with three instead of two cubs in tow, paddled slowly back to Otter Point and hauled out on the rocks close to where she had been lying before. All four shook out their coats – a graceful fountain of

sparkling droplets falling in a shower to the rock and sliding slowly back into the sea. The youngsters pottered about aimlessly for a few minutes, then perhaps tired after the recent stramash, curled all three in a bundle and were immediately asleep. Pinknose sat on a rock close by and started to groom.

The sun beat down on Otter Point but a tiny breeze caressed and cooled the cubs' woolly coats, and they were comfortable. Pinknose glanced briefly at the sleeping trio, then trotted down to the water, breasted in and began to forage in the centre of the Narrows.

In a short while she had worked her way round into Otter Bay. Perhaps sensing her absence, Coll and Cuan woke up, looked sleepily around and realised their mother was missing. Instead of calling her, they rose a trifle unsteadily, seemed to scent her presence in the bay on the far side of the point and set off to join her. Soon they were happily diving into the seaweed forest below and catching themselves crabs, butterfish, and the like. Caorunn stirred as the others moved away but did not wake properly. He tucked his head back into the fur of his belly and resumed his sleep.

Food is never far from the mind of any young otter. About ten minutes later Palethroat's cub, perhaps suddenly sensing himself abandoned, rose to his feet, yawned, looked all round and then began plaintively calling. Even though he was quite a big fellow now, it seemed he was not yet ready to be off and looking for his mother.

Then a strange thing happened. Pinknose came swimming towards the point with a small lumpsucker in her mouth. She made the usual approach dive, rose up through the weed and brought it on to the rock quite close to Caorunn. Instead of eating it herself, or calling to her own youngsters who, perhaps luckily, were out of sight round in Otter Bay, she presented it to the lone cub. She sat nearby while he ate, sprucing up her coat and occasionally yawning.

Caorunn had practically polished off the lumpsucker by the time Coll and Cuan, no doubt looking for their mother, came swimming round from Otter Bay. Arriving at the place where the families so often climbed out on to the rock, they came scampering over the weed to find and greet her. Then they

noticed Caorunn and ran over to greet him, too. Having fed well themselves, they did not seem greatly interested in the few scraps that he had left uneaten. All three cubs began to groom in a desultory fashion and to yawn.

Now Pinknose acted. She rose from her place on the rock, stretched her long body luxuriously, gave another prodigious yawn, then with an air of having all of a sudden made up her mind on something, walked over to a certain place higher on the rock and sprainted. She whickered to the youngsters, and her cubs Coll and Cuan immediately rose up and ran to join her. She ambled off into the nearby wood, complete with family, presumably on her way to a holt that she often used.

Caorunn stayed curled where he was. Would he obey only the commands of his own mother? In a few minutes, perhaps realising he was alone, he was wide awake. We could almost see panic set in as he looked urgently all round and found no other cubs like himself and no mother, real or adopted. He began to 'peep' loudly and plaintively.

Palethroat at the other end of Mallard Bay probably would not hear the wistful calling, piercing though it was. Pinknose did. She came running back from the wood, stopped dead on the lush patch of grass at the top of the rocks and looked down. She whickered when she saw Caorunn scurrying to meet her. She turned at once and he followed her back into the trees.

Ten minutes, twenty, and then thirty went by. No more otters. No Pinknose and cubs. No Caorunn. What of Palethroat? Just as we were deciding that we had missed seeing her go into a holt near Birch Point, evidently quite happy to leave her cub on his own, we saw her slip unobtrusively round the base of Otter Point, in and out of the floating weed, then come out on to the rock. She began sniffing all over it, learned what she needed to know, then followed the trail of the others into the wood.

Again the long pause to see if any of them reappeared. We checked the point and the shores and water on either side of it, but saw nothing. We decided that Pinknose and Palethroat and their cubs were all in the same holt together or curled comfortably in some coorie place in the heather or bracken. They were not likely to move until the tide was running again.

That evening in the caravan I sat writing-up the notes, a long

but rewarding business. It had been a full and fascinating day with no fewer than two 'firsts' to record. Nothing these extremely sociable little animals did would greatly surprise us after so many years of watching them, but we had never before seen one of the bitches adopting the cub of the other, nor the dominant dog feeding one of the cubs. The relationship between the two bitches was friendly and not in the least competitive. In fact, at this stage of the cubs' development they are no longer territorial and each may be found, with their offspring, almost anywhere on the loch that is not too far from the main breeding holts. These will be used by both families as and when it is convenient. On Loch Dorran it was only when the cubs were still confined to the holt or its immediate environs, or were small vulnerable creatures first brought to the shore, that each bitch seemed to keep within a fairly loosely defined territory of her own. This was probably more to do with a reluctance to be far from the youngsters than a need to defend each her own space.

I told Don of my neat and tidy explanation for our inability to find Palethroat and why she had turned up in the outer loch at Badger Bay.

'Certainly, there was a yacht,' was his cautious assessment. 'And I did take a look at that holt near the bay – it's being used. So maybe you're right.'

I was about to ask for his own theory when the cats, The Golden Wonder and Calum Cat, our two most efficient predators, came softly in through the window. Each was carrying a vole, and both were growling.

'Not more!' I exclaimed in despair.

There had been nine victims the night before, four wood mice and five short-tailed voles, and these were numbers three and four brought in this evening. Both cats thudded down to the floor and began the squeaking agony game they always played.

'There seem to be a lot of voles, this year,' remarked Don after we had rescued this particular pair and released them outside. 'Good for owls and buzzards anyway.'

'Yes, and foxes too!' I said, referring to one of our favourite mammals which, in this area, must depend greatly on these creatures for their food. We followed the fortunes of the local pair with much interest.

SEVEN

Placing a Seal On It

THICK MIST enveloped the loch one early morning during the last week of June. The trees in the oakwood above the Narrows were hung with ethereal droplets which fell as light rain on our shoulders. Grass, ferns, mosses, the last of the bluebells, all in our path, shed glistening showers on either side as our wellingtons brushed by. To the east, a pale translucency in the mist suggested the sun might soon part the dense curtains and roll them away. To the west, where we were bound, it was dark and apparently impenetrable.

As we entered the wood and climbed towards the Oakwood Viewpoint a great sound from below began to build to an eerie fortissimo. We paused, as usual, to gaze down towards the deeply enshrouded Narrows and saw nothing, yet out of that shadowed opacity came a chorus of woeful voices, a host of plaintive ghosts all lost and bewailing their lot: '*ohouh, ohouh, ohouh*' . . . where are you? . . . we need you. It was seal pups on Seal Island, calling for their mothers. Intermingled with these pathetic sounds, this mournful cacophony, were the deep grunting replies of the parents . . . we are here . . . we are coming. The annual pupping of the seals was well under way.

'Won't be much otter viewing today,' Don said ruefully.

He was referring not to the mist but to the seals. There seemed to be a great many of them this year and our otters, if around at all, would be secretive and hard to discover.

'Cheer up,' I said. 'You'll be watching seals instead.'

'Yes,' he agreed with only faint enthusiasm. 'See you.'

With that he set off along the path that eventually would take him to Badger Point, and I slithered down through ever-thickening mist and sodden vegetation to the Rock Point watching place below.

Once there, I felt as if I were embalmed in cotton wool. No vision and only the overwhelming, but muffled, sound of the seals. The waters of the Narrows lapped softly and secretly against the skerry rocks below. Gulls floated by overhead, lost in the pearly curtains and speaking *sotto voce* together as from a far off heavenly place. Red-throated divers – abandoned souls, perhaps, in a misty hell – wailed weirdly to each other somewhere out in Matt's Bay. That was all until suddenly, much closer in Mallard Bay, a heron squawked. I heard the laboured flapping of its wings and was immediately alert. What creature could have disturbed it? Was that otter cubs I could hear squabbling?

The plaintive calling of the seals, lost there in the mist, a nebulous echoing of sound round the invisible shores of the loch, was almost oppressive and seemed to taunt a would-be otter watcher, though there was momentary entertainment. All at once a body thrashed down into the water nearby and shock waves from a massive wash slapped and sucked at the rocks below. I imagined a lumbersome bull seal porpoising importantly along, an impressive passer-by I was never going to see. Less romantically, a cheerful robin whistled a tentative greeting to the day in the dripping wood behind me.

The giant rock, my watching place, was cold and clammy to the touch, the ground at my feet a muddy puddle with heather roots breaking through the soil. The mist seemed as solid as ever, and the sound of all the activity going on about me was frustrating to say the least – millions of clinging droplets were all I could see. I glanced hopefully towards the summit of Rock Point. A small rowan sapling growing there was sometimes a useful indicator of changing conditions, and now, as if cautiously to test the air, its topmost branches were poking moisture-laden fingers through the mist and bending minutely to an unseen force. Good. If the sun did not arrive soon to clear the air, then the merest whiff of a breeze might do the trick instead.

Suddenly, from somewhere on the invisible skerry rocks below, came a sound that could not be mistaken, a heavy

grunting, not of a creature in pain but one apparently engaged in a task requiring considerable effort. Heavens! A seal was giving birth to her pup tantalisingly close, and I could not see a thing. Hurry up breeze! It was amazing that the creature had not scented me, and there was nothing I could do now to move out of sight should the mist shortly clear – she would certainly hear me. The only thing to do was to sink as far as I could into the curve of the rock and freeze. Exasperated and fascinated, I listened to the grunts and groans of her labour and then to its sudden ceasing. It was all over, the golden moment gone. '*Ohouh, ohouh, ohouh,*' sang the pups on Seal Island, a welcome to one of their own, but a doleful dirge to match my disgust.

After that of course the mist cleared quickly, as it often does on a warm summer morning. Suffused with the golden glow of sunrise, it began to dissolve into wispy shreds and puff balls, all swirling away into the heavens. Within minutes the sapling rowan had been born from its fluffy white womb and now was silhouetted, clean and bright, against the backdrop of a blue sky. More important, the merest touch on my right cheek reassured me that the breeze, such as it was, came from the south west. My scent could not be carried to the rocks below.

Out of the vanishing shroud emerged a glistening, glowing creature huge and beautiful. A common seal. She lay, pale silver grey, mottled with charcoal, recumbent on a bed of tawny seaweed no more than ten yards away. Beside her, born already in its first adult coat, the umbilical cord still attached and raw, was a much smaller, darker version of herself. The afterbirth, now a useless bloody mess, was spread upon the weed and a pair of great black-backed gulls stood patiently by, waiting to seize and tear. These birds, always in attendance at seal pupping time, stand impudently close and apparently theatening when a pup is being born, or pace up and down watching and waiting. They seem to be concerned only with the afterbirth, however, and the seal mothers take little or no notice of them.

This mother kept turning her head to look at her infant, then humped awkwardly round into a better position to clean it up. The pup lay inert, a sleek damp object with enormous eyes, being prodded this way and that into life. It seemed much darker than its parent, perhaps because it was so wet. The weed, the rock, and

99

the water beyond, was a world it knew nothing of as yet, and bewildered by this strange experience, the youngster huddled close against its mother's ample underside and closed its eyes.

Instead of feeding her pup or allowing it to rest, the seal mother began to nudge it firmly with her nose towards the water. She had chosen a good place for the birth, for the seaweed-covered rock sloped gently to the loch and made a good ramp. Little effort was required as she prodded and pushed, and the submissive babe made no attempt to resist. Slowly and surely it was shunted closer and closer to what, in human understanding, must be a truly alarming experience but to it would be normality. At the water's edge the helpless babe was bundled unceremoniously in. It sank out of sight.

A miracle took place. This helpless object, born but a few minutes before, bounced up through the tangle and at once became a water baby, completely at home. With an easy humping of its body and a flipping of its small hind limbs, it launched itself forward in the water and was immediately swimming smoothly, confidently and entirely instinctively in the shallows near the skerry rocks. The mother humped down into the water after it, hurried to meet it and began gliding alongside her pup. Protective and caring, she turned her head to nuzzle gently and encourage.

They swam effortlessly side by side through the shallow waters, nosing into seaweed clefts and crevices on each skerry, exploring the nooks and crannies of its rocks. Then further out, in deeper water, they danced a graceful seal ballet, the youngster curving silkily over and under its mother's great body, hind limbs flipping, small body drifting, sinking, and rising again. And she responded to its movement, languidly repeating its curving and swerving, rolling over, diving down, rising in unison to swim slowly alongside. Floating over her back, the babe hitched a ride, fore-flippers clinging to her shoulders. It kept falling off, swimming fast to catch up, then gripping her once again. Round and round the pair of them cavorted, halfway to Seal Island and back, the mother turning her head to reassure and check.

A last great circling round brought them triumphantly cruising back towards the birthing rock. A great swelling in the water became the mother and pup majestically rising out of its depths,

to part the weed. The gulls took off, silently peeling away towards Seal Island. There they alighted softly, with speculative eyes, beside another pregnant seal.

The mother seal hauled herself on to the weed and began to hitch laboriously up on to the rock, body humping, flippers working hard. The little one, floating ashore on a ripple, tried its best to follow, but always slid back on the slippery weed to fall again into the water. It uttered no sound of distress, but the mother, ever protective, kept glancing round to check on her offspring. Seeing that it needed help, she humped herself awkwardly round again and started to move back down over the wet tangle to meet it.

At last, they were face to face. Noses met, bristling whiskers intermingled, and no doubt a reassuring message passed from the anxious mother. At once the youngster was trying again. It was an interesting sight, perhaps an example of extreme motherly concern, for instead of humping herself round again and heading up the rock, the mother stayed nose to nose with her infant and, with a great effort, began heaving herself backwards. This seemed to encourage the pup to greater effort. Inch by inch it gained more on each humping than it lost in sliding back, and not many moments later the two of them were lying comfortably side by side in a hollow on the rock.

This hollow, nicely cleaned up by the black-backed gulls, was precisely the spot where the birthing had taken place, and I thought the two would sleep for a while. Not at all. The mother rolled and wriggled over on to her side, thus presenting two bulging nipples to her pup. The youngster needed no encouragement. Nosing urgently into her capacious underside, searching here, searching there, it did its best to find what it so badly needed. The helpless creature became more and more anxious and confused and began moving up the huge body instead of down it. It came to a halt right beside its mother's head – a comic sight, the puzzled, frustrated pup and the exasperated mother. None too gently, the great seal began urging her babe down the long expanse of her belly with her flipper until, at last, connection was achieved and it sucked happily and noisily.

Nearly forty minutes had passed since I had arrived at Rock Point – more than time to check the shores of the Narrows and

Seal Island for otters. Visibility was excellent now, and the water calm. I remembered that sound, heard earlier and lost in the mist, otters perhaps scrapping together somewhere over in Mallard Bay. That was the place to check first.

A small party of otters was indeed there secretly, almost furtively, threading its way through the seaweed shallows of the bay. They swam quietly in and out of clusters of weed, keeping close in to the small rocks that were dotted here and there, behaving altogether as if they wished to draw as little attention to themselves as possible. I could see a large otter and two smaller ones – surely Pinknose with her family. They foraged as they moved along, catching small prey, heads down, forepaws scrabbling at the weed, nosing here, nosing there, into crevices and cracks and, while floating in the water, eating from their paws whatever they had caught. It was a lot of hard work for comparatively little reward, but this was often how it was while the seals were pupping, particularly if there were large numbers of them.

Pinknose – I did get a glimpse of her nose whilst she was eating a crab – suddenly started to swim steadily along, not foraging any more and keeping close to the seaweed fringe where it joined the shore. In deeper water now, she dived occasionally and then popped up to continue in the same direction. Sometimes she checked that her youngsters were with her and they, perhaps sensing what was afoot, tagged along obediently behind. In a few minutes they all arrived at the foot of the Birch Point rocks and hauled out. After giving their coats a shaking, and with no further hanging about, Pinknose led the way into the trees and they vanished.

When, after twenty minutes or so, they had not reappeared, I assumed they were in a holt or sleeping somewhere.

'Do you read me?' came the voice on my radio.

'Sure,' I replied. 'How's it with you?'

'Palethroat has just gone into the holt over here, with Caorunn. They were foraging in Badger Bay when I arrived.'

'Snap! Pinknose and family have just entered one of the holts at Birch Point. Too many seals and bedtime for otters.' I told Don about the seal mother and her newly born pup.

'There are plenty of them over here as well,' he commented.

'On almost all the rocks. No room for otters.'

As we did not expect to see the otters again until the evening, if then, it might be thought that we could have packed up and spent the rest of the day doing something else, but not so. Noting the absence of the creature from the loch, for whatever period, would be as relevant as many an interesting sighting – in this case, typical otter behaviour at seal pupping time. Anyway, it was going to be a lovely day and the time would pass quickly with other creatures to watch instead. Otter Point, Rock Point and the shores on either side of the Narrows each sparkled clean and polished in the sunshine and soon it would be uncomfortably warm.

In the Seal Island nursery there were seals on every available piece of rock, twenty-five adults that I could see, but there would be more round the far side. Seals basking in the sunshine, head-up, tail-up, dozing. Seals awkwardly scratching their sides with energetic, rasping flippers. Seals feeding their babes. Three, heavy and pregnant, were patiently waiting for the great event – one must have been imminent, for two black-backed gulls, softly, softly, alighted on a rock nearby. In shallow water seal pups searched for food and played infant seal games, porpoising along in smaller, less impressive arcs than their elders and slamming down into the water again with what looked like joyful abandon. When tired, they swam to find their mothers, and the air was full of the calling of pups: *'ohouh, ohouh, ohouh'* . . . where are you?

There was a sudden disturbance in the centre of the Narrows between Rock Point and Otter Point, a tumult of churning waters that sparkled in the sunshine. A joyous meeting of otter families miraculously turned up from nowhere? Not at all. Just one! Ahead of the cascading turbulence streaked a small animal, swimming furiously along, diving desperately, swimming again, apparently racing for dear life for the rocks. From what? Behind came a large bull seal, a silver flying torpedo, rising majestically from the water in a graceful arc and slamming down again too close for comfort. Once more the huge creature heaved out of the water to curve over and crash down, desperate, it seemed, to catch the fleeing otter. As the foaming wash came rolling over the Narrows to the rocks below me, Bodach, the big dog otter,

popped up through the weed on Otter Point and hurriedly hauled out on to its rocks. He turned briefly to look at his clumsy tormentor, then nonchalantly, as if nothing untoward had been happening, sauntered to the top. There he sat himself down and began to groom his silky brown coat.

I thought the Big Dog might remain for a while, perhaps to sleep off this exciting experience. Not at all. In only a minute or so, he shook himself again, yawned, and began wandering over the great boulders towards Mallard Bay, sniffing all the way and no doubt picking up scent of Pinknose and her cubs. Finally he added a spraint of his own to one of theirs, then slipped into the water. I watched him skulking along through the shallows, hugging the shore, making use of seaweed cover, but keeping on steadily until he arrived at Birch Point. He came ashore, shook himself thoroughly, and ran up the cleft in the rocks where Pinknose had gone before.

The mother seal had taken not a blind bit of notice when the big bull had cavorted past in pursuit of the otter. But dozing in the sunshine while her pup was still feeding, she spared him a brief looking over when he came sweeping back down the Narrows. He paused in his journey to show off his splendour, curving in the shallow waters round the rocks, swerving away into deeper water, speeding merrily along, and porpoising most gracefully for such a bulky creature. From time to time he cleared his throat, a loud coughing and hawking sound, as if a fish were stuck in his gullet. It seemed he was demonstrating to the seal on the rock what a very fine fellow he was, but he soon passed on, sinking deep in the water on his way to Seal Island and finally disappearing for good.

This behaviour by the males does appear to occur mostly at pupping time and must have some significance. Within a few weeks of their birth the pups will be able to fend for themselves and will have separated from their mothers, who will then mate again. The impressive displaying on the part of the bulls may be a build-up to this, a sorting out of dominant animals over inferior or younger ones.

Suddenly there was action on the rocks below me. Perhaps the mother seal had decided her pup had fed well enough for the moment, or else that it was time to move on. Rudely casting it

off, by pushing it away from her nipple and rolling back on to her stomach, she humped and hitched her way down to the water. At once the little one faithfully followed. They breasted in, one after the other, glided slowly through the tangle, then dived. They did not appear again.

There was no further glimpse of an otter during the rest of the day. When Don joined me, we listened for a while to the mournful music from Seal Island, then set off through the wood for home.

EIGHT

A Fox on the Shore

CAUGHT IN A SHAFT of early morning sunshine, poised on a patch of lichen-covered rock on Birch Point, sat an old friend of ours. With silver birch and bracken camouflage behind him, his tawny coat aflame in the golden light, Reynard the big dog fox was earnestly regarding the shores of Mallard Bay. A carpet of seaweed, brown, orange and yellow, lay rolling away before him and he knew, without a doubt, that juicy morsels beneath its glistening fronds were there in plenty to fill his belly. His nose told him so, and also that there were no enemies about to threaten his safety. He rose from the rock, long and lanky-legged, white-tipped tail flowing out behind, and trotted down on to the shore.

It was the last week of June and six o'clock in the morning. On the way to the shore we had paused at the Oakwood Viewpoint to check the Narrows and had seen the rufous creature at once. A nice start to the day.

'I think I'll come down to Rock Point for a while,' exclaimed Don, whose first love was probably the fox.

'Doesn't he look in terrific condition?' I remarked.

'It's all those voles!' my husband said, laughing as he remembered the exploits of our cats and the inexhaustible supply of their favourite prey that season. 'Come on.'

At Rock Point, first a hasty checking to make sure of Reynard in Mallard Bay – he was still there, just below the rocks of Birch Point – then a look over all the shores and waters of the loch, just in case, in spite of all the seals and their pups, there were any

otters about. The seals were stirring into life, wriggling into more comfortable positions, waiting patiently for the tide to rise and fishing to begin. There was no sign of otters. Knowing well that the loch would soon be full of seals, Pinknose and Palethroat had probably taken their families into their holts. Then a small movement in the shallows of Otter Bay, an unobtrusive humping of the weed, a rippling circle spreading over the water, a long tail waving about in the air, suddenly gave away an otter secretly foraging in the seaweed.

The broad head, bristling whiskers and pale throat of Bodach, popping up with a crab to eat, confirmed our suspicions that it might be him.

'Look who's there!' I whispered to Don.

'I wonder which way he will go,' he said, clearly thinking that the animal might work his way up the loch and perhaps meet the fox in Mallard Bay.

'That might be fun,' was my comment to his unspoken thought, and we smiled.

By this time Reynard was stalking stealthily and steadily over the shores of Mallard Bay towards Otter Point. He was not in any hurry, pottering about in a leisurely sort of way, his inquisitive nose investigating irresistible scents beneath the weed and poking itself into every nook and cranny on the rocks along the way. Dainty paws industriously scraped and parted the tangle, the sharp nose following, to see what might be there. Then he was crouching to the weed, blending with it, and crawling step by cautious step towards some object. Suddenly he was running, kangaroo-jumping and, *plonk*, pouncing on to something that took his fancy. Nothing much so far as we could see, for whatever it was, he missed. A good try, anyway.

Unabashed by this failure, the big dog fox continued calmly along the shore, finding and catching many a juicy morsel. Small shore crabs, tiny starfish, razor fish, eel pout and the like, all would be acceptable to a hungry fox and each bite and quick swallowing gave us nice opportunities to admire his grey-white throat and chest. From time to time he paused to glance all round, sniffing the air carefully, but there was nothing to alarm him. Once he ran up to the wooded edge of the shore, sniffed a few yards along the dried-up seaweed, then squatted and

dropped a scat. Only a few feet on he lifted a leg and piddled. Messages significant to the rest of his world had been deposited.

Meanwhile Bodach had moved into the deeper waters of the Narrows, the incoming tide no doubt bringing in larger more satisfying prey. He was still west of Otter Point, and with Reynard steadily approaching from the other side and a big catch possible that could easily bring the otter ashore, we began to hope for an interesting encounter. For the moment, though, unworried by the seals which were not yet active, the otter was happily foraging and regularly breaking the surface with something to eat from his paws. Sometimes he just lay on the water, paddling gently against the current while he looked all round. Like the fox, he too seemed to be in no hurry.

In Mallard Bay Reynard was now crouching low to the weed near a large boulder. Long body stretched, eager muzzle scenting, something had his complete attention. The magnificent brush began slowly to swish from side to side. Then he was leaping and pouncing. Into a small pool – *splash*! A sparkling fountain rose high into the air and fell back on his tawny red coat. Quite unconcerned, he lifted his head and firmly held in his jaws was a large crab with wildly waving rippers and legs. The creature clawed desperately at the fox's mouth, his muzzle and cheeks, and he dropped it. But only to shake his head in an exasperated fashion. He seized his victim again, and landed it safely on a nearby rock. Daintily, fastidiously, and with obvious enjoyment, he picked the succulent flesh from within the crab's shell, then sat licking his lips.

Just as the fox completed his meal, Bodach caught a large one too, a lumpsucker. He was close to Otter Point and would certainly have to bring this fish ashore there. He dived with the struggling creature, came up with it in the weed at the base of a small gully in the rocks, dragged it safe from the encroaching tide, and got to work. It was a huge fish that would take him some time to eat. The breeze, blowing from the west, would carry his scent, and of course that of the fish, round into Mallard Bay. Surely Reynard could not miss it?

Scent from the fox would waft away up Mallard Bay and give no warning of his presence to the otter – not that it would have greatly concerned him anyway, for the two creatures tolerated

each other and were not generally in competition for the same prey. The fox would not be averse, however, to a nice piece of lumpsucker carrion and such a delicious aroma would certainly have to be investigated. We could yet see the meeting we hoped for.

If Bodach had finished his fish quickly and returned immediately to the loch, there might not have been any further action. But he did not. He was comfortably ensconced in a hollow between two boulders with a bright-bellied victim to tear apart and looked a most contented animal, certainly in no hurry. The inevitable hoodie, arriving to supervise the proceedings, gave him no warning of the animal approaching his rock. In fact, we wondered where Reynard was. One moment he had been enjoying that crab and next time we looked he had vanished. Perhaps he had not scented the otter and lumpsucker, had had enough to eat, and had wandered off into the shelter of the wood.

Or, perhaps he had not! A few minutes passed, then the crow took off with a raucous squawk. From out of the conifer wood on top of Otter Point, a long low rufous body appeared. Reynard stood for a moment, ears pricked forward, tail held low, nose pointing inquisitively towards the Narrows, then began slowly to pad over the grass and heather and on to the lichened rocks. There he sniffed industriously over the rock, seeming to be intent on covering every inch of it, and only pausing to listen a moment and look around. Undoubtedly something held his deepest interest.

He had a problem. His nose told him roughly where the otter was, but how was he to reach it without being discovered? He could not see the animal and huge boulders barring his way were far too steep to scramble over. He crouched low to work it out, his nose twitching busily, his ears pricked. He had it! Slinking back the way he had come, he made further along the point, came creeping through a small gully, then began to edge along an extremely narrow ledge on top of rock that was sheer to the water. He was now stalking into the wind, so his quarry could not possibly scent him.

Lovely scents of lumpsucker and otter encouraged the fox along, but he was an old hand at this game and did not hurry. Each dark paw was cunningly, carefully placed, his belly brush-

ing the rock, his tail, with its tell-tale tip, held low and streaming out behind. The sharp eyes never deviated from a point on the rock where he felt sure he would surprise his prey. The scent was strong. His twitching nose told him he was nearly there. Pricked ears heard the crunching of jaws.

Blissfully unaware, Bodach continued his meal, from time to time pausing to gaze out over the placid waters of the Narrows. The fox crept closer and closer until at last he was hiding behind a tangle-covered boulder. He poked his nose cautiously round its edge. Ah! He gathered himself for a spring and, *whoosh*, it happened. The fox leapt for the lumpsucker. The otter, totally surprised, dropped it, hissed, and leapt backwards. Fox darted in. Otter rushed to grab his fish.

The two met face to face. A tense moment followed while each animal hesitated. Then the fox, thinking better of an easy meal, dropped the lumpsucker, sprang backwards, lost his footing, and nearly fell into the sea. He recovered just in time then, with as much dignity as he could muster, began loping over the rocks towards Mallard Bay. Well, he seemed to say, I wasn't really serious. It was only a game.

Unperturbed by his encounter with the fox, which came all in the day's work, the Big Dog finished off the lumpsucker, rubbed his grizzled chin and gleaming whiskers along the weed and sat yawning. He must have decided it was time to go, for in a moment he rose, pottered over to another rock, sniffed it all over and dropped a spraint. Then he dawdled over the weed and down into the waters of Mallard Bay. We followed him, for the next five minutes, as he swam steadily for Birch Point. Finally he came ashore and, last seen, was climbing the rocks into the wood, probably on his way to a holt. He had fed well. It was time to sleep.

Meanwhile there was no sign of Reynard and we thought he had vanished for good. The tide was creeping in, the sun beginning to warm the day, and in the centre of the loch the dark heads of seals kept popping up and pointing to the sky, breathing in the good air and resting. By now they were really making their presence felt. A great disturbance midway between Seal Island and Badger Point was an argument between two bull seals and it would have been marvellous to be able to see what was going on

in the depths below. All around Seal Island and its skerries, young seals cavorted in the shallow waters, playing strenuous seal pup games or feeding on whatever seafood they could find. Their mothers were never far away and their contact calls, though not so frequent as before, echoed now and again in the still air above the island.

Don had just decided it was time to trek on up to Badger Point, and was yanking his rucksack into place, when the colony of common gulls nesting on Seal Island burst into tumultuous life. The recumbent birds, some on eggs and some with hatchlings, rose with outraged squawking and wildly flapping wings into the air and began wheeling overhead in a whirling, swirling cloud of protest, twisting, turning, stooping and swooping for their nests, skimming the ground then soaring upwards again to repeat the attack. All the while they screeched frantic hate. What was going on?

It was, of course, Reynard! He must have picked up the delicious scents from Otter Point and opted for approach from the cover of the forest rather than the open shore. Now his long lean tawny body was streaking from nest to nest and devouring their contents, eggs and helpless chicks alike. The poor gulls screamed their frustration but were helpless.

We wondered how the fox had arrived on the island. At low water on a springs tide it would be perfectly possible for him to walk across the low seaweed-covered rocks, but we were not into springs, the tide had been rising for at least an hour and there was quite a depth of water in the channel that separated it from the mainland. When he returned, we would hope to catch him in the act.

Reynard polished off the remainder of the nests quickly, running from one to the other with scarcely a pause. He paid no attention whatever to the protesting gulls and his rufous body was easy for us to follow in the short heather and grass. At last it was done. Suddenly, perhaps aware of the encroaching tide, he was running through the vegetation nose to the ground, evidently retracing his steps. Arriving on the high rocks above the little channel, he leapt gracefully down from one large boulder to another, clawing his way over their steep, sheer sides, and landed near the water right beside the nest of a merganser duck. The

drake took off, squawking indignantly, but his lady, sitting tight on her eggs, stayed firmly put.

The fox took no notice of either. He breasted straight into the water and with no hesitation at all began to swim for the other side. We watched, fascinated, the long fox body so buoyant the water reached only halfway up his sides, the thick brush floating out behind, chin and muzzle cleaving a clean course through the water as he paddled hard for the other side. He seemed perfectly at ease, as if he had done this many times before. He probably had.

Landing safely, and completely unruffled by his swim, Reynard gave himself a big shaking out but did not hang around. He trotted over seaweed-covered rocks and bare granite up into the shelter of the trees and disappeared. Four pairs of gulls flew back to the island and seemed to have eggs still to sit on. The episode over, the damage done, they settled philosophically on their nests as if nothing untoward had happened. The rest flew aimlessly about or perched in disconsolate groups on the neighbouring skerries. They would not lay again this year.

It had been a fascinating episode. Though we had always assumed that foxes could swim, we had never actually seen one do so. Now we had proof. Otters are frequently accused of predating on gulls' eggs and chicks, and probably do so when nothing better is available. Here, at any rate, had been an alternative sinner.

'That was fun,' I said. 'Badger Point will be a bit of an anti-climax. Do you think you should bother?'

'Oh, yes,' smiled Don and off he went, knowing it was most unlikely, with all those seals about, that he would see any otters.

That evening, after a long day of otter non-watching and feeling restless as a result, we took the boat over the loch to the other side. We were almost certain that Reynard's mate had cubs and were on our way to a place from which we hoped to watch her den. A gentle breeze was blowing from the west and was perfect for our purpose. Keeping it always on our faces, we walked the long trail to the open hill, through forest rides, graceful larch woods with patchwork floors of sunshine and shade, and finally through the darker green of mature spruce conifer. Once on the hill, it was easy going for a while over

Grooming the pelt is an essential part of the otter's life. The animal's teeth can be seen clearly on the left

Forepaws of an otter, showing size and strong claws

Pinknose comes ashore, shaking out the water
Palethroat approaching her holt near Mallard Bay

Common seal with young pup near Rock Point

The dog fox that regularly hunted the shoreline

A large cub with prey it is well able to catch for itself

Young pine martens scavenging at a feeding place

short-clipped, sheep-and-deer-grazed vegetation with a nice breeze to keep the midges away.

The last part of the climb was slow and careful over the lower slopes of a corrie, and while we followed narrow deer tracks through boulders and heather, we wished we were as slim and sure-footed as they. Steep rock steps through a broken gully, gritty and dry, gained us height, then a long patch of scree, with nothing to hang on to if we started to slide, had to be traversed before we could reach our goal. At the end of all this was a smooth comfortably wide platform of rock with the cliff at its back. This was our watching place.

'Looks promising,' whispered Don, after we had settled down and checked with our binoculars.

Over the centuries boulders of all sizes and shapes, dark and monstrous, had fallen from the lowering cliffs above and been scattered all over the ground in the shadowed corrie below. They were dotted, as well, over the long slope of verdant grass beyond, where wild flowers were growing and red deer often grazed. On a steep bank were three dark holes, each a part of the complex that was the vixen's den. All three entrances were bare of plant life, the ground all nicely padded down and worn. In fact the whole area looked thoroughly used and, best of all, bones were lying everywhere, picked clean and bleached by the sun.

We felt reasonably safe from giving away our presence, being a considerable height above the den and the encircling cliff was so steep it would be an unlikely route in to the den for either of the adult foxes, should they be away hunting. Nevertheless, a tawny streak slinking across the hillside below would send the usual anticipatory shivers down our spines and cause a shrinking against our camouflaging background of rock.

For an hour we listened appreciatively to skylarks singing their evening song and soaring high into a sky turning pink and gold, meadow pipits piping plaintively, wheatears scolding, and a raven somewhere to the west on Eagle Crag calling a gruff good night to its family: '*cruk, cruk, cruk*'. A small group of hinds wandered slowly over the corrie on their way to somewhere else, taking their time, browsing the vegetation, the leader raising her head from time to time to look and listen. They vanished out of

sight across the hill and into the setting sun. All was peaceful.

Action came a little earlier than we had expected. It had been a hot day and maybe impatient cubs, difficult to restrain in a furnace hole below, took matters into their own hands. A small face appeared suddenly against the background gloom of one of the holes, then vanished again as if it had never been. Then there were two at another, a pair of small heads, side by side, poking enquiring noses into the evening air. Greatly daring, they came right out on to the bare ground at the entrance and sat yawning, as if still waking up. They stood stretching small bodies, then turned twice in a circle on the spot, and sat down again. With pricked ears and noses scenting, they seemed preoccupied with something down the hillside and we hoped they were looking for their mother bringing food. Then the two cubs, as if all at once dismayed by their temerity, rose again to their feet and scampered back into the den. Damn, more waiting, and perhaps they would not come up again!

Twenty minutes passed, and then thirty. No rebellious cubs came up to cool off and there was no sign of the vixen. Was she still at home and could our scent be reaching her in spite of all our precautions? It seemed unlikely, but if she was, she would just sit tight, imprisoned below by our presence and later lead her family to another den. That would be a disaster for would-be fox watchers, for who knows to which of several she would take them?

We need not have worried. Only a few moments later, from the smallest of the holes, a cub poked its nose into the evening air and decided it was safe to come out. Right behind and with no delay came another, then numbers three, four and five as well. Five cubs!

While they stretched themselves and yawned the sleep away, we took a good look. Eight or nine weeks old, we reckoned, which was about right if they had been born in April, the usual time for this part of the country. Two were larger than the others and probably male, and one, much smaller than the remaining two, must have been the runt of the litter, unable to win its share of the available food. In the soft evening light their markings were clear and distinct, ears dark-tipped, coats already thick and red and well on the way to adult pelage, and each had a white tip

to its tail. They were beginning to look like proper little foxes and had little resemblance to the small, woolly, dark grey puppy-like objects they would have been at birth.

Before long the fun started and a rough-and-tumble was in full swing. Five young cubs, all working off the enforced inactivity of the day, were chasing each other in and out of the holes of the den and tearing round and round the padded down place that was their playground. It was a hide-and-seek, catch-me-if-you-can, king-of-the-castle kind of a game, boisterous and rough, puppy-dog-cubs leaping, pouncing, rolling over and over, kicking, biting, and squealing at the tops of their voices. It would be strange if their loud rejoicings did not bring an anxious mother.

Ten minutes turmoil – that was all. After that the cubs sat around panting, long narrow tongues hanging out and sides heaving as they struggled for breath. Coats were scratched, bodies stretched, and then they were yawning and, like the otter youngsters so often did, looking around aimlessly for what to do next.

We were so intrigued that we missed the arrival of a shadowy presence which we suddenly spotted sitting motionless in front of the main hole of the den. It was the vixen. She must have been down below all the time. Her stay was brief, however. A command of some sort was given to the cubs, then she turned and, crouching low, nosed her way back into the den. Somewhat reluctantly, the youngsters followed and soon all had vanished into the cavernous hole. It was as if they had never been.

By now the sun had disappeared behind a long ridge. The bird world had retired for the night and no more small groups of hinds browsed across the hillside – they would have gone to higher places to avoid the tormenting midges. Long shadows were creeping over the corrie and a gentle breeze sighed softly round its sombre sides. Soon the den would merge with the hillside and fade into obscurity. Almost inevitably, an owl hooted softly from somewhere in the woods on the other side of the loch, and we smiled at the thought of the cheeky pair which had nested this year in an old tree stump not fifty yards from the caravan.

Out of this thought but still alert, I saw a small movement on the long slope of the hill below. Was it heated imagination or was

that a white blob, the tip of a fox's brush, climbing slowly towards us? I nudged Don and he nodded and smiled.

The dot climbed steadily up the hill, disappeared into tall bracken, and appeared once again in a patch of grass. Now the whole of the creature could be seen. The white dot, of course, was on the end of a long bushy tail, the tail on the end of a long rufous body. Our dog! Even in this light we recognised the sheer size, the long legs, the magnificent head and that particularly luxuriant tuft of white on the end of his tail. Reynard.

The fox was carrying what looked like a hare in his jaws and now he began to act cautious. At the bottom of the corrie, he dropped his burden, raising his head with ears pricked and nose pointing, to check that all was safe. We cringed at the thought of an unexpected down draught from us to him. He found nothing to alarm him, however, picked up his prey and began to tread delicately up through the scattered boulders of the corrie. Soon, he reached one of the holes of the den.

He must have called for, in only seconds, a face, momentarily motionless in the shadow of the hole, became the vixen scrambling out to meet him. There were no fond greetings. The dog dropped the hare at his feet and immediately she snatched it away, turned on the spot, and without a backward glance, dragged the bloody prize below. The dog fox, apparently taking this ingratitude entirely for granted, loped off with an air of having satisfactorily done his duty and disappeared into the all-enveloping gloom. In the den, no doubt, there was a great squabbling and squeaking, a tearing apart and a greedy munching. The cubs had probably not had any food for some time.

We crept away. It was too dark to see any more.

Next morning, very early, as if to round off the evening before, we watched the dog and his vixen together hunting the shores of Mallard Bay. They prowled slowly over the glistening carpet, nosing here, nosing there among the boulders and seaweed, and seemed to be finding plenty of prey. They were never far apart, but in a little while the vixen trotted off towards the wooded edge of the bay and disappeared into the trees. We imagined her hurrying over the steep hillside. She would not leave her unruly cubs for too long and soon would be chasing them down into the safety of the den.

NINE

Marten Magic

FROM SOMEWHERE in the wood at Rock Point came an unearthly screaming, an agonised caterwauling as of some creature being done unmercifully to death.

'Have you brought the polecats with you?' teased Don over the radio.

He was at Badger Point as usual and I at Rock.

'I'm beginning to wonder!' I exclaimed as the raucous sound continued. 'I'll get back to you.'

At one time, I had bred these delightful little creatures with the aim of producing an animal as close as possible to the true polecat, which is now extinct in the Scottish Highlands. The mating occasions of my pets had been rough and rude affairs with a great deal of noise to accompany the act. The savage squealing, now lifting out of the wood behind me, was indeed reminiscent and must be investigated at once.

During a sudden pause in the cacophony, and afraid I was going to miss seeing the creatures, I crept as quickly as possible and not too carefully along the ledge which led from my watching place to the back of the big rock buttress. The silence continued and I stopped to listen and look. Nothing. Were they already gone? Had I been in too much of a hurry?

To my great relief, the screeching started again. Cats fighting to the death? No. Otters squabbling? Definitely not. But it certainly sounded like two creatures having a serious disagreement. Then right in the middle of a bed of wild iris, only about thirty feet away, there was a rustling sound and a disturbance that

caused their leaves to wave wildly all over the place. Two dark furry bodies with long bushy tails burst clear of the vegetation and appeared to be locked in mortal combat.

Pine martens! Not polecats. At that moment they were engrossed in their savage love-making and completely unaware of my presence. A cruel business it seemed to be. All raw and bleeding, the female's neck was firmly gripped in the teeth of her mate. He was dragging her about all over the place, and she, inert and seemingly helpless, was making no attempt to escape. He shook her, bit her, let her go, leapt after her, pounced and held again, and covered the length of her slighter body with his own. It was not to be wondered that she was doing all the screaming.

Maybe, if I had been less careless, it would have ended in a true mating, the two of them remaining tied for some time. In the excitement I had completely forgotten the wind. The evening breeze, though not directly behind me, must have filtered round the great rock buttress towards the animals and carried a whiff of my scent to them. The result was dramatic – instant cessation of a passionate affair. They sprang apart, both animals looking my way. For a second they hesitated, then, as one, broke away from the iris and were bounding for the nearest oak. In a series of graceful leaps, sharp claws tearing the crusty old bark, they streamed up its ancient trunk and at a safe distance, each on a different branch, paused to look below. To my surprise and delight, evidently feeling secure in their leafy haven, they stayed there just watching, waiting perhaps to see what I would do.

It was a marvellous opportunity to examine the beautiful creatures. Chocolate brown coats were thick and shining. Long bushy tails, lying along each bough, twitched gently from side to side. Dark triangular faces, with small rounded ears edged in pale fur, were turned towards me and two pairs of bright enquiring eyes twinkled inquisitively down at me. Most striking of all, against the colour of their coats and the green of fluttering oak leaves, were the beautiful peach-coloured patches which spread over their throats and down on to their breasts. The evening breeze, whispering through the leafy canopy above, gently ruffled the glossy fur of the graceful creatures and I wished the moment would never end.

Suddenly a wretched blackbird called sharply from some-

where nearby. It had probably discovered the martens, not me, but the strident protest had the same predictable result. Startled, both glanced quickly to a holly bush then back again to me. The female, more timid, decided it was time to go. She took off at once, running sure-footed along her branch until she came to its end where she leapt, a graceful arc of gleaming fur, to a sturdy bough on another tree. The bough bent with her weight, bounced up again and took her in another flowing arc to a higher branch on the next tree. And so on, never clumsy, never stumbling, in and out of the sunshine, vanishing in shadow, quicksilver movement in golden light, and always making in the direction of the ancient trees high in the wood.

Her bolder mate seemed to be not unduly disturbed by my presence and was still on his branch. He regarded me calmly, not inclined to move. Whether my binoculars bothered him or he became aware of his mate's disappearance, I have no idea, but all at once he too decided to go. He took off, and following roughly the same Tarzan route as the female, leapt gracefully from branch to branch and tree to tree towards the top of the wood.

The female must have been waiting, hidden in the leafy canopy, for one marten became two, a larger and a smaller, dancing effortlessly from one old oak to another, stem to stem, bough to bough, in and out of the patchwork light on the foliage. I lost them at last in a tree-top fastness somewhere near the end of the wood. The charming idyll was over.

The first realisation of the presence of pine martens in the area had come with the discovery of their droppings, or scats. These were found neatly placed on rocks, on roads, paths through the woods, and especially on the tops of the many old walls, or dykes, which transect the hill. These last seem to be a much-used and eminently logical route for the animal between one location and another and are used by other wild creatures as well.

From time to time we had sightings of martens – long, low, mustelid creatures suddenly on a path in the wood, slipping away through the vegetation into a drain or ditch, or leaping up the nearest tree. A male on the hillside, surprised by our German Shepherd dog, leapt squirrel-like up the nearest tree and settled on a branch to await our departure. A small female carrying a vole in her mouth scurried over the rocks near Rock Point. A

male, out hunting, trotted the length of an old dyke from wood to shore. And so on. But this was the first time that either of us had witnessed mating behaviour.

When at last I got back to my radio, I called Don. There was instant and impatient response.

'What have you been doing? I've been trying to call you. Look at the loch beyond Badger Bay.'

I did, and gasped. In the glimmering distance, in water calm as the proverbial millpond, a flotilla of familiar red heads was steadily advancing over the loch. Red deer hinds, nine of them! They seemed to be making for the broad estuary of the Allt nam Bratan, the stream of the salmon, and must have left the shore a little beyond Badger Point. They were a lovely sight, in line astern behind their redoubtable leader. I imagined their slender legs paddling briskly away below while v-shaped ripples spread over the surface, fanning out into one as the still waters were spread apart.

The deer neither hesitated in their purpose nor paused to rest, just swam steadfastly along not even turning their heads to look round. They were approaching the opposite shore when their leader, the matriarch of the group, deviated slightly from her intended route, swam deliberately left, then straight for a few yards, then right again to resume her original course. Had she caught a whiff of some alien scent, or was there a large rock hidden in the shallow water below? Whatever it was, her sisters behind, each in turn, copied her example and then were neatly lined up once again.

They all arrived safely on the other side and rose majestically out of the water to shake huge showers from their bright, russet coats. There was no pause to recover from their arduous journey. The matriarch immediately led the group daintily, prettily, away over the rough pebble shore to sweet pasture beyond. There they came to rest and began to graze.

'That was beautiful,' I enthused to Don a minute or two later. Then I told him about the martens.

'You have all the luck,' he grumbled. 'Listen. I think we should pack it in for tonight. Don't forget we have a visitor coming.'

'I bet he'll be interested in my marten,' I teased.

*

It had all begun some time before. There had been inquiries from Central Television concerning the possibility of making a film about our otter study. We thought about it long and hard, made many telephone calls and asked a lot of questions. Neither of us was sure we wanted to make asses of ourselves in front of a television audience of wildlife experts. Above all, we needed assurances that our otters would not be disturbed. In the end, the project went ahead and the film, if successfully made, would appear in the popular ITV 'Nature Watch' series.

Much of the filming was to be done by a camera crew from Central but it had been hoped that Don would also be able to secure footage of otter 'happenings' to fit in. Unfortunately the equipment he owned, or was able to borrow, was unsuitable. Though many hours were spent on the shore and some good action with otters obtained, the material did not come up to standard. A well-known and much-respected professional wild-life photographer, Eamonn de Buitlear, was engaged and it was he who was paying us a visit.

In fact we did not meet Eamonn until the following day. He had agreed to come at short notice and he and his son Cian, who acted as his assistant, had thrown all the equipment into their vehicle and had driven from Dublin to Loch Dorran in a single day – a long distance. When they failed to turn up at the expected time, we thought they must have decided to spend the night elsewhere and went to bed.

'You must be Don and Bridget,' a gentle Irish voice greeted us when we walked along to their cottage in the morning.

'When did you get here?' we asked guiltily.

'Late! Don't worry, we saw the caravan curtains were drawn.'

We chatted over a mug of coffee and got to know each other a little. Eamonn and Cian were a great pair, enthusiastic about otters and conservation in general, and full of stories of previous experiences. That was fine, but my tidy eye noted a confusion of gear, cameras, tripods, bags, boots, and all sorts of other bits and pieces, lying higgledy-piggledy all over the floor, and I wondered a little at this apparent lack of organisation. It seemed like a casual approach to the work in hand.

I could not have been more mistaken. These two, who always spoke to each other in Irish, could hardly have been more

dedicated, professional and determined to achieve what they had come for, whatever the cost in long hours of discomfort. Just show them where otters were, they would do the rest! And in this connection, of course, lay our worry. It was not the best time of the year for seeing otters. The loch was still full of seals, both adults and pups, and the otters would continue to behave rather secretively. Would we, in fact, see any?

Eamonn and Cian soon finished off their breakfast and were ready to start. The idea was to walk along the shore, chat about regularly used rocks and points and choose vantage positions from which filming might be done. Points Badger, Marten, Rock and Rhuaidh were obvious locations. Eamonn had already done a lot of work with the animal in Ireland, so that was a great advantage. He would certainly know the difficulties involved. Always prepared for action, he had brought all the equipment they might need. Don noted with satisfaction, and a little envy, the Arriflex camera which he knew would have excellent lenses and be almost silent when in action.

The sun was shining, the day warm and Loch Dorran was looking its sparkling best. We walked along the shore into a gentle breeze and noted Eamonn weighing-up the various locations with a professional eye. He seemed to like what he saw. Finally, hopeful of an otter or two passing by, we left them at Rock Point, a position recommended by Don for its close proximity to the Otter Point 'stage' and enthusiastically approved by Eamonn. After walking away we turned for a moment to see what they were doing. Eamonn was crouched beside his camera and Cian was examining the loch with his binoculars.

'They looked happy enough,' I remarked as we arrived back at the caravan to grab a bite and give the dogs a short run.

'I hope they stay happy,' replied Don gloomily. He meant, of course, 'Let there be otters!'

Fifteen minutes later, while we were sitting eating a sandwich, there came the sound of a motor, startling in the midday stillness, revving up in the direction of the Big House. This was where Cian had parked their vehicle.

'What on earth!' I exclaimed.

In a few more seconds their smart white van came roaring past

on the rough Estate road below, bouncing over the potholes, skidding in and out of the ruts, and going a lot faster than was good for it. What could be wrong? What had happened? We thought of driving over to the cottage to see if help were needed.

The cloud of dust had barely begun to settle when the van was tearing back again, mission accomplished. As it turned out, there was no disaster. This frenetic journey, made each morning our visitors were with us, was Cian rushing back to collect their lunch. We never did work out why he couldn't have prepared the food before they set off in the morning and taken it with them. Perhaps he needed a break.

As assistant to his father, Cian was always well laden, and we sometimes wondered how he managed. On each trip there would be a heavy rucksack on his back and an even heavier tripod over one shoulder, and sometimes he had recording equipment with him as well. An inspiring sight was the two of them setting out through the wood or across the shore, Eamonn slim and slight, his yachtsman's cap at a jaunty angle, and Cian, more stockily built, marching resolutely along behind, his red head bare whatever the weather. Both would be watching the water and the shore with an eagle eye, alert for the slightest suggestion of action.

We got a good routine going. Most often, Eamonn would be at Rock Point hoping especially for action on Otter Point. From there he was able to move quickly westward along the shore towards Badger Point or eastward through the Narrows, should it be necessary. The day began as soon as the light was good enough for filming. Don started at Badger Point and usually joined the other two after a while. I stationed myself at Rhuaidh Point to cover the Narrows, Birch Point over the way, and Matt's Bay. We both had radios and were able to make our way quickly to Eamonn if necessary.

The days seemed to race by too fast. The weather was the usual West Highland summer mix, bright, still, overcast, showery, breezy, the midges appalling when it was humid, and tending to be awful whenever there was a good chance of filming otters in action. Being used to similar conditions in their own country, the Irishmen took it all in their stride. The seals were a problem, as expected. Long hours were spent examining the shallows along

the shores, looking for any furtive movement which would give away a skulking otter in their midst.

One day we had a bonus. Reynard the fox, our beautiful boy with the tawny coat and luxuriant brush, arrived on the shore. It was almost low water and once again he appeared at Birch Point and began prowling across the broad seaweed carpet in Mallard Bay. Once more the action was fairly predictable, a great help for someone trying to make a film. The fox strolled in a leisurely fashion over the shore, scenting the tangle, parting it daintily with inquisitive nose or paw, then pouncing on the prey that was hiding beneath. He covered the whole of the bay, taking his time, and we wondered if he would also come on to Otter Point as he was in the habit of doing. I held my breath. It could be a beautiful sequence.

Our fox took his customary route, vanishing into the forest at the west end of the bay then making a cautious appearance from among the trees on the top of the Point. Satisfied all was well, he came out on to the rock and stood poised in all his rufous glory, surveying the scene around him. From Rhuaidh Point I could see Cian laying down his binoculars, checking the lens on the camera and standing by to assist if necessary. Eamonn, cap pulled low on his forehead, was crouching behind the camera and lifting his hand to make an adjustment. When the film was eventually completed, a charming little sequence of a fox hunting over the shore and appearing on Otter Point was included. Success.

In spite of all the difficulties, Eamonn had more luck than we had dared to expect and was reasonably happy with the footage he managed to get. By the sixth day, however, he was still without a good close-up of Pinknose with her cubs. That would be the icing on the cake. All we needed were the right conditions, good weather and light, the otter with her cubs on rocks where the cameraman could be within reasonable range and some interesting action. Not much to ask.

The plan was the same as always – there was no better one. Don walked down to Badger Point, Eamonn and Cian prepared for filming from Rock Point, and I remained at Rhuaidh. It was not a promising day, overcast so that the light was not at its best, and a brisk breeze from the east ruffling the loch into little white horses, which would make it difficult to discover otters, in the

water anyway. The Narrows were so sombre I wondered whether there was light enough even for Eamonn's wonderful camera. I watched him and Cian arrive at Rock Point, erect the tripod and fix the camera. Then they were sitting quietly close-by and using their binoculars.

An hour and a half passed and no otters obliged us by putting in an appearance. Perhaps our doughty cameramen would give up. A small flotilla of mergansers sailed by, two ducks with eleven ducklings in all. A grumpy heron in Mallard Bay stood patiently waiting for the tide to bring it a meal. The few gulls remaining on Seal Island after Reynard's depredations flew busily back and forth from the loch, presumably attending to the needs of their chicks. Most of the seals on the island were hauled out and languidly watching pups in the water – the mournful sound of their calling an appropriate accompaniment to forebodings that there would be no otters.

I saw Don joining Eamonn and the three of them chatting together. Then three faces were watching the water and Don, still looking, was lifting his radio to his mouth.

'Your sympathetic otter spotter here,' he joked. 'There's an awful lot of nothing except seals in these parts. How about you?'

'Ditto,' I replied. 'The water's so choppy here I'm afraid of missing something. How are those two?'

'Cheerful, as ever, and optimistic,' he laughed. 'Cian is thrilled with the sound of the seal pups calling. He's going to record them.'

'At least you've got something going on,' I complained.

At that moment, as if on cue, one dark otter head, then two more beside it, popped up through the weed in the shallows off Birch Point. They had arrived without my spotting them, presumably straight from a holt. Now they were foraging. Nerves began to tingle all down my back. This might be the start of the action we were hoping for. I willed the little group to be Pinknose and cubs, though really they were most unlikely to be any other combination of three.

What would those otters do? Stay where they were and retire back into their holt when hunger was satisfied? Make their way down over Mallard Bay and oblige Eamonn by hauling out on Otter Point? Cross over the loch and come ashore right below

the eager filmers on Rock Point? There were several other options, but I willed them to do just that, for it would be a great climax for the Irishmen. I wondered whether they had noticed what was happening up my end and was just about to radio the good news when I realised with horror that I had managed to lose my otters. In choppy water, so easily done, and done too often. Frantically I scanned the deeper water, then searched the shallows and the rocks on the shore. Not a sign. One minute they were there, now they were gone.

Ten minutes passed with never a sighting, and then came the shock. Suddenly, in the bay west of Rhuaidh Point, three otters could be seen sailing in through the choppy water, follow-my-leader-like, towards the rocks. Now lost in the white horses, now calmly riding down a wave into calmer water, they were swimming steadily towards me. How could I have missed them? They came joyously gliding in on a crest, dived one, and two, and three, then popped up in the shallows. There, in amongst the tangle, they began to forage.

I seized my radio. 'Are you there?' I inquired urgently.

'Why not?' my husband mocked.

'No time for joking,' I replied. 'Pinknose and cubs are in Rhuaidh Bay. At the moment they're foraging.'

Don did not bother to check with his binoculars. He recognised the significance of this news at once. The family would almost certainly come ashore either with a big fish or for a quick grooming and rest. Either action would make a nice little sequence for Eamonn.

'Okay. We'll come as quick as we can. Tell that otter bitch not to be in such a hurry!'

The wind was still from the east, so it was perfectly safe for them to come by the shore. I watched Don slithering down the steep rocks at Rock Point and begin dancing over the boulders towards me, a journey made so many times that he could make it surefooted and fast. Eamonn was right behind, treading lightly and delicately over the slippery seaweed and doing almost as well. Cian, carefree as ever though hindered by his heavy burden, brought up the rear, yet somehow he was managing to keep up with the others.

But would they come fast enough? By this time Pinknose had

stopped foraging and, ahead of her cubs Coll and Cuan, was swimming purposefully towards Rhuaidh Point. Don came to a sudden halt, turned hastily to gesture and whisper to the others, then crouched behind a boulder waving them forward. At the same moment Pinknose came sailing serenely in to the rocks on the east end of the Point. Coll and Cuan were close behind her. They would all come ashore at any moment.

I discovered with dismay that most of the action would be taking place out of my sight behind the tall rocks of the point. The top half of Cian hurriedly erected the tripod and placed the camera on its top. Then he was sinking slowly down beside his father, who was already crouched and prepared for action. Both were almost lost to me and for the moment I could only guess at what was going on.

Suddenly Eamonn's hand came up to pull his cap lower over his face, a sure sign of tension, and he sank even closer to the rock. Then his hand was up again, desperately trying to adjust the lens. He seemed to be trying to wrap himself round the tripod legs, presumably in a hopeless attempt to be behind the camera. Undoubtedly *something* was happening!

Suddenly I realised that the camera was now pointing west down the loch and I knew that the otters had sailed past Eamonn and were away. This would make any return to the point impossible, for they would at once pick up the human scent. I saw Don lifting his arms to heaven in mock despair and almost at the same time Pinknose and family swimming and diving fast across the Narrows towards Mallard Bay. Curtain!

Poor Eamonn was mad at himself. 'Oh, Lord!' was all he actually said out loud, but he was clearly upset. 'I had the wrong lens on and no time to change it. Never thought they'd come so close.'

The only thing to do was to laugh. Anyway, he should not have been blaming himself. How was he to know that the wretched creatures would almost walk over his feet.

'Cheer up,' I comforted him. 'There's a nice surprise for you this evening.'

Jean Hornsby, who with her husband Mick ran the holiday cottages on the estate, had been putting out scraps every day to attract a pine marten mother with kits. The marten was coming

quite regularly to the bait and taking food across the burn and into the wood where her family waited. We thought Eamonn would like to try for some film of her.

That evening a band of hopefuls each selected a strategic position from which to set-up and use his equipment. Eamonn had pride of place with his tripod and camera. Don stood close by to advise on likely behaviour and also, with tripod and camera, to try for some stills. Cian had brought recording equipment along to catch sound of the marten kits squabbling, and his camera as well. Most important of all, I had brought the raspberry jam!

Jean had been putting out any scraps that became available. The disadvantage of this for would-be photographers was that the animal would come for the food, stay only briefly, then vanish with its prize to the hungry kits nearby. We wanted the marten mother to remain put for a while and perhaps for her kits to join her. The jam, which of course could not be carried away, might do the trick.

It did. About half an hour later a little face appeared beneath a nearby oil tank, the mother's usual method of approach. She paused for a moment, looking cautiously round and scenting, then, satisfied all was well, and seeming to be quite unworried by the strange pieces of furniture all dotted about the clearing in front of her, advanced towards the enticing aroma of raspberry jam. At once she was totally absorbed, appreciatively licking away at the stone upon which it was smeared.

There was much squeaking among the trees across the burn, her impatient family wondering when she would come – we are hungry, hurry up and bring the food. I saw a couple of shadowy creatures streaking down the stem of a birch. Kittens! The mother stopped licking, turned for a moment to look, then ran back the way she had come. Would she bring them to the bait?

In only a few seconds the family came into sight. At first they followed tentatively from the darkness beneath the tank, one, two, and three kits, each a small replica of its parent. Then all three came scampering after their mother, to investigate the sticky red stuff on the stones. She sat watchfully by, and they licked happily away. It was all great fun and the session only ended when the family had finished the jam. They ran back

across the burn, into the trees and disappeared for good up a gully.

There were several more attempts at marten filming before Eamonn and Cian left for home. The animals became so used to us they took no notice of anyone walking quietly about to focus lenses, put out more jam, and so on. Eamonn shot some excellent material, Cian recorded some nice marten 'squabblings', and Don took some good stills.

The last day of the visit arrived and, by and large, it had been a success. Now it would be for the Central Television crew to come and do their bit in November. So as to be ready for an early start in the morning, Eamonn and Cian packed their van the evening before – it was to be home to Dublin in one if at all possible – and came to the caravan for a little ceilidh. They walked up from the road to reminisce a little on the adventures of the week and to say goodbye. We sat companionably together, mugs of coffee on our knees, discussing the events of the week. At last, the moment came for parting. Eamonn, with great deliberation, placed his mug on the table and with an air of something important still to be done, put his hand in his pocket and drew out with a flourish a gleaming mouth organ.

'We'll just have a little music before we go,' he smiled.

The instrument was carefully polished with his handkerchief, then lifted to his lips. Just in time, I surreptitiously pressed the record button on the mini tape recorder. After a short warming-up, the caravan was filled with the sound of a haunting Irish air, a lament to suit all partings, a sad farewell to a pleasant occasion. Shian, the collie dog, cocked her ears, heaved a deep sigh, then settled to sleep again. The cats looked startled and fled through the caravan door. Dirky, the big German Shepherd, lifted his voice to the heavens and howled a wolflike, melancholy accompaniment.

We were sorry to see them go. It had all been great fun.

TEN

Catching an Image

A LL WILDLIFE photographers are mad, but some are more mad than others, especially if they are naturalists as well. Though intimate knowledge of a creature's way of life and behaviour is a great help in the business of obtaining pictures, it also inspires an almost obsessive ambition to achieve the unusual, or indeed the unachievable! Don is one of these. Discomfort and long hours mean nothing to him and the subject set up in artificial circumstances is of little or no interest. As complete a record as possible of the otter's way of life in the wild is his chief concern.

There are all the difficulties that might be expected in the business, but light – that elusive quality which is never right just at the hoped-for moment – is the main bugbear of the otter photographer. On Loch Dorran, and probably in all coastal situations, this animal is about at any time of the day, but dawn and dusk are the favourites when it can go quietly about its business undisturbed. That, of course, is when the light is at its worst and most difficult for the camera to handle, at least as far as colour photography is concerned. Imagine trying to separate a dark brown animal from the seaweed with which it is perfectly camouflaged and against a background of sparkling water! From late autumn through to early spring the problem is compounded, in these parts, by a sun which is low in the sky.

It was already September and this season's cubs were growing up fast. Palethroat's Caorunn was about nine months old and Pinknose's Coll and Cuan about eight. Soon it would be more difficult to catch family groups together. The youngsters would

often be acting independently of their mothers, and the bitches might soon be pregnant with the next lot of cubs. Don needed more of these pictures if possible. Also, still eluding him was that glorious moment – the ultimate in otter photographs – when the dominant dog would be caught exchanging greetings with one, or even both of his families together.

Since July, and Eamonn de Buitlear's visit, we had been watching otter activity as best we could. Towards the end of that month, when the young seal pups were already more or less independent of their mothers, pressures from that quarter became less. But there were others to take their place. Human beings. More and more people take their summer holidays on this lovely west coast, and with the tourists come fresh difficulties for the wildlife photographer. Not only does the subject again become an elusive creature but heart-breaking moments occur when, against the odds, a good otter picture is possible and suddenly there is scent, sound or sight of visitors approaching along the shore. *Pouff!* The perfect photograph has vanished.

Don had no assistant to carry his gear and my job was to help find the subjects. His first move in the early morning was to peep through the caravan curtains. No point in lugging a great load of cameras, tripods, lenses, spare film and so on all the way along the shore and back if there was not enough light or the weather conditions were hopeless. This morning, however, when he hoped to capture one or both of the family groups, was perfect – almost no breeze, the mist rising away from the loch and promise of sunrise quite soon. We dressed and breakfasted quickly, let the dogs out for a run, and were soon standing beside the loch working out the best plan for the day.

From what point should Don start? The wind was always the most important consideration, for a whiff of human scent could cause no action at all or, worse still, the most perfect of pictures to vanish suddenly. To which side of the loch should he go? His best chances would probably occur on the other side because that was where the greater part of otter activity took place. The tide had been ebbing for a couple of hours, so large expanses of seaweed would soon be the perfect stage for action.

'What do you think?' I asked Don as we stood there for all the world like a pair of otters scenting the air.

'Well, what breeze there is is from the south west, so I'll need to work down the shore from wherever I start. The other side, I think. Pinknose was over there yesterday.'

'Okay. What do you want me to do?'

'Go to Rock Point and I'll walk up to the fence. From there we will be able to see each other. We'll use the radios. Any messages gratefully received!'

He meant, of course, news of otters seen from my vantage point which would be out of sight to him. I looked at the usual heavy load.

'Will you manage that lot in the boat?'

'No problem. It's nice and calm.'

We parted and, if all went well, I would arrive at Rock Point a little while before Don reached his highpoint at the fence on top of Birch Point. This would give me time to check all the shores, particularly those on his side. I was having, as always, those nasty feelings that the tiresome creatures would choose to come ashore on my side of the loch, or beautiful action was already in progress somewhere suitable but with no time for the photographer to arrive and catch it. There is a lot of luck in this business.

Rock Point was much as usual for this time of the morning, still in shadow and cold, and it would be a little while yet before the rays of the newly risen sun reached over the loch to warm it. At least there were no midges. A preliminary check over Mallard Bay, Birch Point and Otter Point revealed nothing unusual and no otters. The inevitable gulls swooped and soared above the loch, stretching their wings after the long night's roosting. A raft of merganser ducks bobbed bravely on tiny wavelets across a golden shaft of sunlight. Two cormorants were fishing in the Narrows below and I imagined their swift movement below the surface, darting here and there, long necks extended, webbed feet speeding them along to catch their prey. Sentinel herons were spaced out along the shoreline in their favourite fishing stances. One, perched on a rock halfway along the broad reach of Birch Point, could be a nuisance. If it suddenly discovered the patient photographer sitting nearby, an angry squawk would give the game away.

At last I heard the sound of a motor, hardly audible at that distance and with the breeze blowing it away. White foam from

the wash of the inflatable, fanning out and fading away on the water, confirmed its passing. Then the engine was cut and I knew that the boat would be silently drifting the last few yards towards the steep shelving rocks on the far side of Birch Point.

Another wait now – for action that today I could not see, but with unnecessary concern could imagine only too well. Don would have to get himself and all his gear ashore. The ebbing tide meant a boat constantly dragging away from the ledge on which he must land, and the seaweed, only recently uncovered, would be wet and slippery. A long leap was necessary, nicely judged over water at least eight feet deep. I could never forget that my husband could not swim, but it did not seem to worry him. So far there had been only minor disasters.

It was impracticable to anchor the boat and wade ashore because, if he were a long time away, it might well be floating on a risen tide well out of leaping distance when he returned. Conversely, if he tied it to a rock on the shore where he landed, and came back quite quickly, the boat could be stranded by an ebbing tide. A long rope brought on to the rocks of the point was the answer so that the boat could float at all times and be hauled in when required. This also allowed Don to hold it close while he yanked his equipment ashore.

Today all appeared to have gone well, for twenty minutes later I picked him out with my binoculars, beautifully anonymous in camouflage clothing, his rucksack on his back and the tripod over his shoulder, arriving at his vantage point. Then the aerial from his radio was glinting in the sun as he raised it to speak.

'I'm here, in case you've not noticed,' he said. 'Is there anything?'

'Not at the moment,' I replied.

'I think I'll wait here for a while. Don't want to spoil my chances by getting ahead of the wind.'

'Right. It all looks good and the light is going to be lovely.'

'Yeah. Let there be otters!'

While we waited for action I thought about the various options open to Don. He could stalk down from the fence and arrange himself in a suitable position above the shore, birches and heather for background, and wait for otters, as it were, to come to him. They could either arrive on the rocks below from a holt, and with

133

luck stay a while, or else they could come ashore from the loch, conveniently within focusing range, and be photographed maybe eating a big fish. Either of these could easily occur, but there was always the tiresome possibility that there might be no otters around to oblige. Much valuable time could be wasted.

Another option was to go looking for the animal, stalking always into the wind, across Mallard Bay. If they were conveniently at its east end and making their way west, this would be hard work, for Don would have to keep pace as they foraged along the shore, always watching that he did not get ahead of them and so be scented. He would move only when the creatures had dived, guess where they would come ashore, and hope that they would not double back when out of sight under water. To the comfortable watcher, it might all be hilarious, but to the photographer it was a laborious gamble. To add to the permutations, something exciting might suddenly happen on Birch Point. That would involve making a long detour into the woods in order to avoid being scented and then, maybe, arriving too late. A philosophical attitude is required on these occasions.

The third course for Don was probably the best – to stay put at the fence and rely on information from me. I could see nearly every foot of the shore on the other side, all of Birch Point except the steep rocks in Matt's Bay where the boat was secured, the whole of Mallard Bay and Otter Point, and so on to Seal Island. If it all happened near Seal Island the only decision he would have to take would be whether to stalk all the way there (an arduous business with all the gear) or wait and hope the animals would eventually work much closer to him. It helps a lot if you know the habits of the creature.

In a short time we had action. Pinknose suddenly appeared with her two large cubs near one of the skerries on the east side of Seal Island. They were all happily foraging and must have recently come from a holt nearby. By now, a certain pattern of behaviour had been established by this bitch. At some time, probably within the last twenty-four hours, she would have left a holt near Birch Point and gone foraging with the family all the way down to Seal Island. There, eventually, they would all have entered another holt. Probably to fit in with the tides, she would then have worked back again to Birch Point, feeding on the way.

She was perhaps in the process of doing this now, but it could only be guesswork at this stage. I was more concerned about cloud which had appeared in the sky to the south. Would it arrive and spoil chances of photography altogether? Should Don come quickly and hope for a picture? I decided to have a word.

'There's nothing happening up here,' he replied to my news. 'I think I'll gamble on them coming to Otter Point. You can watch me along the shore and when I'm near the end of Mallard Bay I'll get in touch.'

'Suppose they nip quickly past. They'll get your scent then.'

'I'll risk it. The light is good at the moment.'

I hoped there was enough time. The first part of Don's journey, from fence to shore, was over terrible ground – deep ditches full of water, bog nearly all the way, and a gully to scramble over with slippery boulders and a tumbling burn. Instinct had prompted him to come, however, and he was a glutton for punishment. My job must be to keep an eye on the otter family.

They, the blessed creatures, were right in the middle of one of their energetic romps and were still close to the nearest of the Seal Island skerries. They should be happily occupied for a few minutes longer. It was the usual noisy robust affair, dashing in and out of the water, chasing each other, with occasional pauses to roam about on the rocks, sniffing for scent and sprainting. It was a good opportunity to see how the cubs were progressing, and it seemed well. Two well-grown youngsters, nicely fat and rounded, were fast catching up their mother in size, and Coll, the little male, was already quite markedly larger than his sister and more chunky in build.

Too soon, Pinknose made up her mind to move on. She broke away from her family and began swimming in the direction of the Narrows. I do not know whether she called, but quite soon Coll and Cuan were paddling briskly after her, probably following her scent on the ebbing tide. This did not augur well for Don. Though all three foraged through the little bays between Seal Island and Otter Point, they were coming too fast. At the moment only halfway across Mallard Bay, he would have to hurry if he was to be there in time. I wondered if he had left his

radio switched on in spite of our agreement not to speak. It was worth a try.

'Do you read me?'

I saw him pause and reach for his pocket. Out came the radio. 'Yes?'

I told him.

'Okay. Thanks.'

The radio was hurriedly replaced and I watched him running and stumbling over the slippery weed as fast as he could. There was quite a way to go.

Pinknose and family had now arrived in Otter Bay, still foraging. I watched them anxiously, willing them to catch only small items of prey which would be eaten from their paws in the water. A big one would be brought ashore in the bay and would almost certainly mean appetites satisfied and Otter Point bypassed on their way to Birch Point.

It was while I was anxiously watching the family that the next complication occurred. Another otter! A big fellow that could only be Bodach, the dominant dog, was swimming round the far western point of Seal Island and making for the skerries. Perhaps he would pick up the scent of Pinknose and her cubs and join up with them? Could the picture Don was after, above all others, be within his grasp? I wondered whether I dare speak to him to warn him of the possibility.

The enthusiastic photographer was working his way along one of the ledges on the steep east side of Otter Point, a sheer fall to deep water on his right and a higher parallel ledge covered in vegetation on his left. His tripod was held precariously over one shoulder, the rucksack on his back and his spare hand was feeling for any holds it could find on the way. Not the moment to call! He arrived at last on the nose of the point, a broad platform of rock quite high above the water, and began to ease the rucksack from his back.

Pinknose chose this moment to catch the big one. I saw her rise triumphantly from the deeper water in the Narrows, held my breath to see which way she would go, and then watched her swimming towards a tiny skerry below Otter Point which was only clear of water at spring tides. The blessed angel! That ought to suit Don if he could get into position in time without giving his

presence away. The cubs had realised instantly what was happening and were trying to grab what they could from their mother.
They would all come ashore together. I must speak.

'Can you hear me?' I whispered, turning my head away from
the loch and hoping no sound of my voice could reach out over
the water.

'Yes.'

'Keep your voice down. Pinknose and family are on their
way to the skerry just below you, with a lumpsucker and – wait
for it – Bodach, on his way from Seal Island, is hurrying to catch
them up.'

'Oh, God! Right. Shut down radios and wave yours if there's
anything urgent. I just might see you.'

'Right. Good luck.'

It would mean a lot to Don if he could get that picture.
Pinknose with Coll and Cuan would be lovely, but a group with
Bodach included as well would be special. Feeling utterly useless,
I watched anxiously from Rock Point.

Don was edging forward carefully on his rock and down closer
to the water, still in sitting position and dragging the rucksack
and tripod after him. Pinknose and family came sailing in to the
favourite rock and between them the fish was dragged on to its
seaweed top. Then all three were shaking themselves out. Don
was having a problem with a tripod leg which would not anchor
on the smooth rock surface – so no picture of otters in a cloud of
sparkling droplets!

The family started to tear and eat in the usual unmannerly otter
way, disputing each bite and whickering with excitement. The
photographer was frantically screwing the camera on to its tripod
and adjusting the lens – no picture of squabbling otters either,
unless he hurried up. To crown all, Bodach chose this particular
moment to pop up right in the centre of the Narrows between
Rock Point and Otter Point.

I saw Don glance my way – no question of using the radio this
time. I could only point towards the Big Dog, stick my thumb in
the air and hope he would get the message. He nodded and
smiled, then I saw him crouching low on the sloping rock,
waiting, willing, hoping.

Unpredictable otters! Pinknose suddenly picked up the scent

of her mate. Instead of continuing with her meal she dropped the fish at once and, with the cubs faithfully following, scrambled into the water and set out to meet him. All of them dived, and then there were four otters having a terrific greetings ceremony and romp in the middle of the Narrows. Not very photogenic, unfortunately, and not at all what Don had wanted. But there was still hope. When the rumbustious game was over, they all might come swimming back to Otter Point and haul out on the little island. Don had evidently decided this too, for he was cautiously edging himself, with the camera, further down the rock and much nearer to the water. The risk of discovery would be greater but the picture, with a much larger image, would have been worth the gamble if successful. I knew he would be willing them to come ashore all at the one moment and at the same spot as before.

Of course it did not happen that way. After a few minutes, the Big Dog decided it was time to go. Instead of coming on to Otter Point, the wretch began immediately to swim up the shore on my side of the loch towards Rhuaidh Point. Pretty soon he picked up Don's scent, dived and was seen no more. Pinknose swam back to her unfinished meal and the cubs quickly followed her.

The fish was quickly demolished and the family went into the usual routine of grooming, energetically scratching, rolling on the weed in the small space available, shaking themselves out and finally, as if tired out with all their activity, curling up to sleep. In a small hollow in the weed, the fur of one big and two small otter bodies rose and fell with their breathing.

The little islet was beginning to disappear, but the photographer seemed unaware of the advancing tide. The otters stirred every minute or so, as otters do, to scent and look around. The tide was of little consequence to them, but to Don, as close to the water as he could possibly be, it would be of much greater interest, especially if the tripod and camera fell in. So engrossed was he that I was sure he had not noticed what was happening.

A few minutes later Pinknose rose, stretched and yawned, then slipped quietly into the water only inches away from where she had been sleeping. From the centre of the Narrows she whickered to her family but they – perhaps tired with all the activity and with fine fat meals inside them – responded drowsily to

her call and began swimming in the opposite direction across the tiny gap between the skerry and Otter Point. Coll came gliding ashore and started to climb the rock. Intent on catching up, Cuan came leaping and scrambling after him. Totally unaware of the photographer's presence, they both ran, one after the other, straight through the legs of the tripod and over his knees. They halted in shocked surprise, hissed a startled protest, then ran for their lives down the rock and back into the water. I saw Don swivelling the lens round, desperately trying to catch the golden moment, but they were far too close, and besides, he was roaring with laughter.

The cubs met up with their mother in the Narrows. They all dived immediately and – entirely predictably – disappeared for good. I turned my binoculars back to Don. He was scratching his head and regarding his trousers with comical dismay. Not only was his lap covered in soaking, otter-smelling water but the rising tide, unnoticed while he was concentrating so hard on photography, had crept up the sloping rock over feet and ankles, and was now halfway up to his knees. When he was safely back on the top of Otter Point I called him.

'That was nice. Are you going swimming?'

'Not just now. A shame about Bodach,' was his rueful comment.

'Never mind. At least you haven't dropped the camera in the loch!'

'I might detour into the wood and see if I can catch up with them in Mallard Bay. That family are sure to work along the shore in the shallows.'

'You'll be working with the wind,' I protested.

'Well, I'll just need to keep ahead of them.'

At least his trousers are wet already, I thought resignedly. It was not unusual to see a camouflaged figure, leaping over a seaweed shore, carrying a ready set tripod with camera on top, watching the water with eagle eyes and sometimes crouching to take a picture. Almost certainly, at some point, he would be kneeling in the advancing tide or squatting in a very large puddle.

'Tell you what,' he went on, as if reading my thought that he was probably wasting time and energy because the otter family had fed well and probably would not bother to do much

foraging, 'I'll detour to Birch Point. Maybe they'll all come ashore there.'

I knew he was hoping Bodach would miraculously join the party again. I thought it unlikely. In fact, Pinknose and family arrived at Birch Point long before Don, who had to make that laborious journey through the bog. They disappeared straight into the trees on their way to a holt. In any case, the threatening cloud from the south was now almost overhead and the light fading by the minute. We agreed it was as well to pack it in for the day. I sauntered back along the shore whilst Don was making his way to the boat for the return trip over the loch.

Nowadays there is a wide choice of equipment for the wildlife photographer but the noise made either by the camera shutter release or an attached motor drive is a problem as yet largely unsolved. These sounds are instantly picked up by the otter's sharp ears, though there are some, like Bodach, who may eventually become quite used to them. Because of the weight factor involved when stalking, the 35mm camera with motor drive is almost obligatory, for telephoto lenses from 400mm to 600mm are needed and must be carried as well. There are cameras on the market now, however, with a built-in drive and these are quieter. The perfectly silent reflex camera has still to be invented.

There are many fine makes of camera but over thirty years ago Don invested in Nikons and has remained with them ever since. A reliable camera is important, but more so are good lenses. The very best of these are usually beyond the pocket of the average amateur photographer and this penalty has always applied in his case.

Infinite patience, unquenchable enthusiasm, and a certain capacity to endure everything from biting winds to hordes of midges, are attributes needed by the wildlife photographer. In his everyday life, Don is not notable for the first, but when pursuing this favourite of tasks he seems to have endless reserves of all three. Three or four hours at a time are routine but often it is a whole day of watching and waiting. There are dismal failures and heartening rewards. Sometimes he gets a good one!

ELEVEN

Otters as Film Stars

WE HAD NO IDEA what to expect. It was late one afternoon in March when a young, strikingly attractive figure came walking slowly up the path to the caravan, looking all around her and pausing from time to time to inspect more closely some object that had caught her attention. We had thought someone older and somehow more formidable would be coming.

'Hello,' she said with a smile as the dogs rushed to greet her while we stood at the caravan door. 'I'm Tish Faith.'

With steaming mugs of tea we sat by the picture window, admiring the view, but there was no hanging about, no relaxing after a long tiring journey. Our director got straight down to business.

'How long have you been doing this?' she asked.

'Coming up eight years, but only the last four intensively. Since I retired,' Don replied.

We had imagined a pleasant hour getting to know each other, then we would give our visitor from Central Television a cosy meal and send her early to bed after an exhausting day. Instead, the questions came pouring out and we found Tish easy to get on with. I was on the point of offering our enthusiastic guest a glass of sherry when she closed her notebook briskly and replaced it in her briefcase.

'Right,' she said. 'That was lovely. Now we'll go and look at the loch.'

'Don't you want to see your cottage first and settle in?' I asked in surprise. This young lady had just flown from London to

Glasgow and spent six hours at the wheel of a car to Loch Dorran.

'Later,' she said pleasantly. 'Let's catch the last of the light.'

'We'll only be half an hour,' Don said at the door as he saw my anxious glance at the half prepared food.

The passage of time and eating were both of little consequence to Tish. It was more than an hour later before I heard voices approaching over the field from the wood.

'What a wonderful place!' she said with unconcealed delight as they shed jackets and boots at the door. 'I've brought a video camera with me, so I can get some shots of you here in the caravan and record an interview. Tomorrow I'll shoot something of the loch for Robin to see.'

'Robin' was Robin Brown, the Producer of the whole 'Nature Watch' series, whose consent would be required before serious filming could go ahead.

'Would you like to eat first?' I suggested hopefully, thinking of my casserole simmering on the caravan cooker.

'No,' she replied without hesitation. She must have no sense of smell, nor an appetite, I thought. 'Let's get the work done first,' she said cheerfully.

The camera Tish had been issued with for the occasion was one she had not used before. Instead of a brisk interview and a few minutes filming, she and Don settled down with some hand-written instructions to start putting the thing together from unassembled pieces they found in its case. Then they had to discover how it worked! This setback did not seem to worry our director, nor for that matter Don who loved cameras, but the cook was in despair. Half an hour passed before they were ready to start filming. It was all pleasantly relaxed and we found it easy enough to tell Tish about our work. We learned a little, too, of how the filming would be done and what would be required of us.

At last, after a late supper that miraculously was not ruined, Tish decided the day had ended.

'Thanks for a lovely meal,' she said sweetly. 'Will you show me an otter tomorrow?'

'You will need to be up early,' I said.

'I'll be ready.'

When Don returned from escorting our seemingly tireless guest to the nearby cottage where she was staying, I asked him if she was settling in all right.

'I suppose so,' he replied doubtfully. 'She's busy writing up notes. Do you think she ever stops?'

*

Next morning we assembled in front of Tish's door at first light.

'Does it always do this?' she inquired with a smile.

On a day when we were hoping to show her the place at its most beautiful, the sky was overcast, a fine smirr of rain was falling and a brisk breeze beginning to blow from the east. That could mean white horses on the loch. If we hurried to Rock Point we might manage to find an otter for her before it became too difficult to see one. But if we had already learned that Tish was a workaholic, we were now to discover that in no circumstances could she be hurried. She sauntered happily along the Estate road, admiring the landscape and asking a torrent of questions while she gazed out over the loch with a dreamy expression on her face. As we crossed the fields and entered the woods she frequently stopped to look thoughtfully at some spot that took her fancy. She was not, however, simply admiring the beauties of nature but planning locations and action for the film, a composer composing a symphony, a poet a poem. I was anxiously watching the weather. The water in the Narrows was already becoming rough, wind against tide, and soon there would be no chance at all of spotting an otter. We tried to step up the pace. It was no use. One step at a time seemed to be our director's philosophy – there was all day in which to see otters!

At last we arrived at Rock Point, and if it was atmosphere Tish wanted, she certainly found it there. The buttress rock loomed sombre and forbidding in the steady drizzle. Otter Point on the other side was barely visible. It was all gloom, doom and dripping moisture, and not at all what we had planned. We placed her in the best position for viewing and told her where to try looking. In spite of the foul conditions, Tish happily got busy with Don's binoculars while we peered into the gloom scanning every likely rock and expanse of water, anxious to come up with the goods if we possibly could.

Half an hour passed slowly by while the weather steadily worsened. The binoculars became useless, all smeared with raindrops. A few gulls, calling mournfully to each other, glided through the mist overhead and two cormorants dived energetically after a meal in the waters of the Narrows.

'Have you had enough?' I asked hopefully.

'I'm fine,' replied Tish cheerfully.

At last she was rewarded. Suddenly, out of a rippled circle spreading over the water in a sheltered place below us popped the head and shoulders of an otter with a crab in its paws. None of us had seen it coming. It had probably sneaked round Rock Point close in to the steep sides.

'Look, Tish. There!'

She picked up the animal at once and nodded with pleasure at seeing it. With her eyes still on the otter, her hand went darting to her pocket and out came a camera which was quickly focused. Click, the picture was taken.

'Tish!' Don protested. 'You haven't a hope in this light and with that lens.'

'Never mind,' she replied, unabashed. 'It might just be a recognisable dot. Then I can prove to Robin I've really seen an otter.'

In spite of a good wetting in the morning, Tish wanted to reconnoitre the shore below us after lunch in the caravan. She was after more locations that would be suitable for filming. Don accompanied her and I agreed to join them after taking the dogs for a walk. The rain was now belting down, and I wondered how even the most powerful imagination could possibly envisage the place in sunshine or as a suitable place for making a film.

Half an hour they had said, but an hour passed slowly by. I sat in the shelter of the eves of Tish's cottage and became first fed up, then worried. Where had they got to? Was one of them hurt? I decided to go in search of them with the dogs – their noses might be useful! Eastwards along the loch, they had said.

I found the two of them soon enough, barely three hundred yards along the shore, huddled beneath an overhang of rock on Liath Point and only partially sheltered from the teeming rain. Oblivious of time and the appalling weather, they were happily discussing otters, photography, and plans for the film.

Rainbow over Rock Point

One of Pinknose's cubs, at about two years of age

An injured otter, later found dead

This male otter may take over the range when Bodach is no longer dominant

With television producer Tish Faith and presenter Julian Pettifer on film location

Bodach with prey, beginning to show his age

Bodach grips Palethroat's neck as he attempts to mate with her. Then he climbs on to her. Afterwards the pair enjoy mutual grooming – something frequently carried on by siblings in the same litter

'You can't hurry Tish,' Don said, laughing, when – back in the caravan on our own – I protested.

'I'll Tish her,' I said rudely.

It had been a whirlwind visit by the end of which I was feeling a little frayed. When she said she had seen and heard all she needed, she swept away in her hired car, promising to be in touch again as soon as Robin Brown gave the green light for her film.

*

Soon certainly meant soon. A couple of weeks later a phone call from Tish confirmed that the filming would go ahead in November. Only from a casual remark at the end of this news did we learn that she was expecting a baby in December!

The months passed surprisingly quickly, with the usual routine of work and Eamonn de Buitlear's visit to film otters, before November arrived and once again the tall figure of Tish was climbing the path to the caravan door.

'Hello,' she called cheerfully. 'How are you?'

'Fine. What about you?'

'Doing well,' she said with a grin, glancing at her modest bump. 'How are the otters?'

We were able to tell her that old Bodach was still patrolling up and down his range and that we often saw Pinknose and Palethroat, sometimes with, sometimes without their cubs which were now almost as large as their mothers. There ought to be good opportunities for filming.

'Great. Come and meet everybody over at the Big House. You know we're renting it? Jean Hornsby is going to be looking after us.'

Earlier we had watched a Land Rover and two cars negotiating the ruts and potholes on the road below. The afternoon was drab and grey, the loch looking far from its best. Apprehensively we walked across with Tish to the Big House half a mile away. What would these people be like, who came from a totally different world?

All was utter confusion. The porch was a jumble of wellington boots, waterproof over-trousers and jackets. These overflowed into the entrance hall where suitcases, bags, rucksacks, camera cases and tripods seemed to occupy the entire space, while the

huge sitting room appeared choc-a-bloc with video and record-ing equipment, canisters of film, notebooks, clipboards, clothing, magazines, and people. In the middle of this amazing collection a baby sat placidly on the floor surrounded by toys and an admiring audience.

During the whole of their stay we were never to see the house in any other state than this. But once out on the job, order prevailed and the routine rolled smoothly along. They were a friendly crowd and managed, as well, to give us the impression that they were really interested in otters, in Don and me, and in what they would be doing. Nothing was too strenuous for Tish, nothing too tedious, and the weather was never impossible. Yet, as we were to learn all over again, she was not one to be hurried.

We were introduced to the older team members. Noel, the cameraman, was blond, wiry and looked very fit, and his assistant Ken was tall and shy. Vaughan, the sound recordist, spoke quietly, as if he were always carefully measuring sound levels against intrusive noises. Charming but briskly efficient Bryony, the assistant producer, seemed to combine several administrative jobs and, with the help of her husband and her mother-in-law, looked after her babe as well. The programme's presenter, Julian Pettifer, wouldn't be arriving until next morning, Tish explained. 'He's been held up somewhere.'

'Are you keeping as well as you look?' I asked, curious that she should look scarcely pregnant at all.

'Fine. The baby's kicking nicely.'

We didn't stay long. While we stood in the porch, chatting about plans for the following day, cheerful light from the house was highlighting a heavy drizzle, the sparkling curtain of rain-drops effectively screening the dark world beyond. A phone call to the Glasgow Weather Centre had forecast at best showery days to come, possibly with periods of continuous and heavy rain. Just what was needed!

Tish was undaunted. 'We'll start tomorrow about nine,' she said firmly. 'Eilean Beag with you, Bridget, and Julian. Otter tracks and signs. We've hired the Estate launch and Mick Hornsby will take us down. If Julian hasn't arrived by then, would you, Don, wait behind and bring him in your boat?'

*

I awoke with mixed feelings. The morning was dull but a breeze from the east was already blowing the clouds apart. As we sailed down the loch a grey drab scene became a bright panorama of deep blue choppy seas, autumn colours above the seaweed shores, rugged outcrops, and cliffs of dark rock. Eilean Beag, the little island where we had discovered the live-trapping cage when we first started our study, was a jewel.

The launch, beautifully handled by Mick, was too large to bring close in to the rocks of the island. Everyone aboard and all the baggage had to be transferred into a dinghy and rowed ashore. It was no small task with a south-easterly blowing and a heavy sea running. Once on the rocks at the bottom of the little geo – always the best way to come ashore on the island – the heavy gear had somehow to be dragged or carried by hand, or lifted precariously on to shoulders, while its owners sought blindly for footholes up the rock. We wondered how these people, so awkwardly burdened, would manage up its perpendicular sides. But they all made it safely.

I stood at the top of the geo waiting for Don and Julian to arrive. There was scarcely time to look round this perfect setting for an otter to be filmed before Tish called me. No time was wasted and while the camera crew was sorting out its equipment we walked the familiar track along the northern edge of the island. Clipboard in hand, she planned the action, stopping to consider various vantage points and careful to avoid stepping on the valuable 'evidence' that Julian and I would be going to 'discover'. The sequence began to take shape in her mind, while I found myself manically rehearsing the answers to imaginary questions.

As we were retracing our steps towards the group at the top of the geo I heard the steady hum of Don's boat bouncing over the loch and knew the action was about to start. There were two people on board and butterflies took over in my stomach.

Don brought the boat neatly into the geo and tied up. A tall, blond, extremely fit-looking man was agilely climbing the rock. By now, I was utterly convinced I had not a word to say and knew nothing whatever about otters.

'This is Bridget MacCaskill,' Tish said briskly to Julian. 'Bridget, this is Julian.'

'So, you're the otter people,' Julian said with a smile as Don joined us.

In his role as wildlife presenter, this man had travelled the world, seen just about every impressively large wild animal that existed, yet he confessed he had never seen an otter in the wild. He hoped we could produce one for him, and was certainly keen to learn more of the animal.

'Right,' said Tish. 'Jules, will you come with me. You, too, Bridget. We'll go over the first sequence.'

Again we walked the northern edge of the little island, Julian asking the questions, Tish explaining what she wanted, the two of them planning what would be pointed out and discussed. It was all very professional, with nothing left to chance, yet when filming was in process it would have to appear natural and unrehearsed. I was greatly impressed by the care and thought which went into it all.

We were back at the geo and ready to go. I noted with despair that clouds were now massing together, the sunshine about to disappear.

'Okay Julian?' inquired Tish.

'Sure.'

'Right. Action.'

I heard Ken, a faraway voice as in a dream. 'Take One.'

'Well, Bridget,' said Julian as we set off through the heather. 'Tell me about this island.'

All knowledge of Eilean Beag vanished instantly. I knew nothing and was unable to speak. As my mind raced and the others watched and waited, the hushed silence was loud in my ears. A voice called sharply, 'Cut.'

I was about to apologise when I noticed Vaughan examining the sky. A tiny sound from out of the clouds was steadily approaching – aircraft engines. We waited for it to pass over and I breathed again.

I did a little better when we set off for the next take. No doubt Julian was used to dealing with amateurs for he was easy to talk to and seemed interested in the subject. It was fascinating to watch Noel, Ken and Vaughan charge ahead of us with their gear and be in position for the next sequence long before I had gathered my wits together after the last. The track was narrow

and rough, but no one seemed to get in anyone else's way.

We duly 'discovered' otter spraints and discussed them, noted food remains and talked about what otters ate, looked at a 'coorie' place in the heather where an otter had rested and a holt wherein it was possible there was an animal at that very moment. It seemed to go well enough. By the time we were returning to the top of the geo, however, the wind had increased, the cloud was grey and dark and we peered through a steady drizzle. The light was going. Typical Loch Dorran weather, of course, so the film would be nothing if not true to life.

'Right,' said Tish serenely. 'That's fine. I think we'll get a nice bit of atmosphere now. How's the light, Noel?'

'Just possible,' he replied, a little reluctantly I thought.

'Okay. Don and Bridget. Can you get to that rock down there by the water and appear to be watching otters?'

'Tish,' Don objected. 'No one would ever try to watch otters with this sort of sea running.'

We had a steady downpour now and white-topped waves were rolling into the geo below, slapping up its steep sides in impressive clouds of spray. The long rake of rock – that favourite way for the otters in and out of the loch, where the live-catcher cage had once been set – was extremely slippery. Don stayed upright and trod delicately down its perilous length, but I unashamedly edged slowly down on my seat. At the bottom we sat side by side only inches away from the hungry waves. Water seemed to be everywhere, driving in horizontal sheets out of the leaden sky to meet the spray from the sea, streaming in rivulets down the slope on either side of us and advancing inexorably up the rock on the rising tide. Obediently we scanned the water, apparently deeply interested in something that was not there. It was curious to feel a part of the whole battered scene, at one with the assaulted island. Some atmosphere!

On the other side of the little inlet, a bedraggled group got on with the job. Noel, balancing precariously on a rock, one leg in the sea, was trying to focus his lens. Ken was hovering anxiously by, one arm holding an almost uncontrollable umbrella over the pair of them, the other securing one leg of the tripod. Vaughan, also under an umbrella, was protecting his equipment as best he could and no doubt trying to make the roaring of the elements

recordable sound. Bryony was dutifully writing up continuity notes within the shelter of her raincoat. Julian was looking mildly amused. Enough is enough, he might well have been thinking. Tish, safely back from the slippery rock, seemed totally absorbed in the action and oblivious to the unpleasant conditions.

It was done at last and a hurried packing up began. As Tish and I stood at the top of the geo, awaiting our turn to make the somewhat hazardous climb down into a restless dinghy, I thought, only six weeks to go – a great day for pregnant ladies, this!

'How are you doing?' I asked, anxiously.

She laughed, knowing at once what I meant.

'I'm fine. Don't you worry.'

Eamonn de Buitlear had obtained most of the otter material needed for the film, but this crew would be looking for any special moments with the hope of good footage of Julian discovering his first wild otter. With this in mind, we were all to be prepared to drop everything, at any time, in order to secure the golden event. The sequence would then be fitted into the story wherever suitable.

To our great pleasure, it did actually happen, but not quite as anyone expected. The very next morning we took Julian to our watching place at Rock Point where he and Don were to have a general discussion about otters and then to go on to talk about how we set about studying them. At an agreed moment I was to call them up on our two-way radios from the other side of the point and report an otter coming their way. By the time I arrived, ostentatiously tucking my radio back in my pocket, an otter would obligingly appear – if not for real, then added later from Eamonn's footage or from library film. It would be spotted by one of us and pointed out, with great satisfaction, to Julian.

All went well, and having been recorded giving them my important message, I was duly filmed arriving at Rock Point.

'How close is it now?' asked Don, entering into the spirit of the game and preparing to 'spot it' and point to an empty space.

'Just the other side of Rock Point, in Marten Bay,' I dutifully replied.

'So, Don,' said Julian, continuing to play his part, 'we hope an otter is coming our way, but are there other signs we could be looking for, to give us a clue to their whereabouts?'

'Why, yes,' replied Don, as rehearsed. 'If there's a gull or a hoodie perched on a rock, looking interested in something going on quite close to it, there's sure to be an otter there eating a fish.'

'Right,' said Julian, and we started looking all round with great interest for a non-existent otter.

Tish called, 'Cut. That's fine,' she said. 'Lunch now.'

We were all relaxing and pulling out lunch boxes from rucksacks when there was a sudden hiss from Julian. 'Hey!' he whispered conspiratorially. 'Is that an otter? Over there?'

He was pointing across the Narrows. Feeling slightly foolish, for our roles had been reversed, I looked hastily in the direction he indicated but could see no sign of an otter.

'You're right!' Don exclaimed. 'Well done!'

It was Bodach, the dominant dog of the range. Noel and Ken sprang into action, swivelling the camera round to focus on the creature. Vaughan picked up the mike, and once again we three began enthusiastically discussing the typical behaviour of our favourite creatures. The Big Dog foraged for us along the shore between Otter Point and Seal Island, where he finally disappeared from sight. So we had discovered a real otter after all.

A blustery but reasonably bright morning turned into a much more ominous afternoon. Cloud was building again from the south, the wind rising and the loch becoming rough. The prospects were not good, and when Tish suggested shooting at Suicide Point we thought she was mad.

'It's going to get a lot worse,' Don told her. 'You heard the forecast.'

'Oh, but it's often wrong,' she replied, optimistically. 'I think we should have a go.'

Suicide Point got its name because Tish, on one of her exploratory trips to find suitable locations, had slipped there on some moss and Don had only just managed to save her from a nasty fall.

We battled along the shore, leaning on the wind and envying the camera crew their use of the Land Rover to travel by way of the fields above the wood. For a fleeting moment, the sun highlighted the woods in their autumn colour against a loch that was a deeply ruffled indigo blue dotted with white, the crags

behind in sombre shadow against bright golden light. Lovely atmosphere, but the wind was still rising and the cloud would soon be blotting out the sun.

We scrambled as best we could over great boulders to the perch Tish had chosen. I noticed Don looking anxious.

'What's the matter?' I asked. 'Don't worry about Tish. She'll look after herself okay.'

'I'm thinking about the boat. It really should have been brought ashore when we finished this morning.'

The little inflatable on its mooring would happily ride almost any sea and, if it filled with water, would still stay afloat with the outboard engine quite safe. I did not know that Don had switched our outboard to one of the Estate boats before filming; in a storm, these took in a lot of water and were not stable.

The session had to be aborted after all. A hastily rehearsed interview with suitable background and surroundings was blown away by the wind and there were no breaks in the cloud to stop the relentless rain. We huddled beneath our waterproofs in the partial shelter of the hillside and thought ruefully of the calm quiet weather conditions we had promised Tish.

When, in a comparative lull, we made a dash for home along the shore, Don came hurrying past me.

'I'm going to see if the boat's all right,' he shouted. 'Meet you back at the house.'

As it happened, the boat had turned right over and the outboard fallen to the bottom. Luckily the engine had not parted from its rope and Mick came to the rescue. Once they had the boat righted (no mean feat in that sea) they managed to haul it up. All that was missing was the cowling. Mick made a splendid job of washing out the engine with fresh water and, with coaxing, it eventually sparked into life. It took many hours of work, however, before it became its usual reliable self.

By the next morning the gale had blown itself out. The sun shone on a world sparkling and fresh and the loch was settling down nicely. We did not, however, repair to Suicide Point. In fact we never went back to it at all, for Tish had a timetable to keep. Don was to be filmed next, apparently deeply involved in trying to photograph an otter.

This filming of imagined events was an aspect of the business

which we found amusing and slightly disconcerting, but eventually came to terms with it as a perfectly valid method of making a film. After all, you could not sit around waiting for actual happenings; film-makers who did that might find themselves on location for ever. Provided it was action that repeatedly occurred in reality, it was fine by us.

There was one more surprise to come. As I sat comfortably on a rock, watching Don stalk along the shore in the bay between the Big House and Lodge Point, I heard someone come running up behind me. It was Jean Hornsby.

'Bridget,' she panted. 'There are three otters playing on the sea fence at the top of the loch. Thought you'd like to know.'

The animals must surely have been driven that far up the loch by the weather, for it was unusual to find them there. It sounded promising for a nice little sequence of an otter family doing something different. I hurried back to the car and drove faster than was good for it on that rutted road to a wooded point close to the top of the loch. The fence would be just below. Peeping cautiously through some branches, I saw the family at once – Pinknose, Coll and Cuan, all having a wonderful game of king-of-the-castle on the glistening seaweed which draped its trellised spars. While Pinknose stayed firm on her spar, an upright at her back, one of the cubs tried to dislodge her. Each in turn received a hefty swipe from her paw which sent it tumbling into the water. They loved it. Each fallen tightrope artist, undaunted, climbed on again from deeper water further along, and returned for more. These cubs were now large, but still they could not dislodge their mother. As usual, loud whickering proclaimed their excitement to all within earshot. It was a charming scene.

I dashed all the way back to fetch Tish and found them still busy on the shore.

'Tish,' I panted. 'There are three otters at the head of the loch having a terrific game on the sea fence. What do you think?'

She did not! Don was getting into position for a retake of the action and she was busy checking notes on her clipboard. I do not think she even heard my announcement. One thing at a time was obviously this director's rule. Though disappointed, I realised of course that she was right.

*

To fill in missing bits and pieces and to tidy up loose ends, a second visit was needed. When eventually they all arrived, we discovered a different camera crew – Pete, who (Don always maintained) stood nonchalantly on one foot whenever he was filming, and Garry his assistant. Sue replaced Bryony and this time the baby present was Tish's. Julian was as charming and interested as ever.

It all went smoothly. The interview at Suicide Point was at last achieved and, much to my relief, the sequence on Eilean Beag reshot so that I appeared less nervous. We watched video film and recorded a 'voice over' commentary. The climax came in an altogether unexpected way.

Imagine the caravan, the dogs shut safely away in the car to make more room, the cats fled from their beds; Julian, Don and I sitting uncomfortably close together on the window bench, a small table in front of us spread with maps, photographs and notes; Pete, Garry and their gear crammed into the corridor space, and Vaughan balancing himself and the recording equipment precariously on the dining table turned upside down. Tish, serene as ever, was supervising from somewhere behind Pete. An interview was in progress.

Just as we finished, Julian picked up what looked like a piece of camouflage netting from the cushion beside him.

'What, on earth, is this?' he asked, curious.

'Come outside and I'll show you,' Don replied with a chuckle.

When Tish and I heard the roars of laughter, we ran out to see Julian prancing in and out of the trees, waving his arms like an enormous bat, the voluminous folds of Don's portable hide streaming out behind from its coolie hat support on his head. An enormous creature from who knew where!

'You haven't seen anything yet,' I said. I ran back into the caravan and returned with two strange contraptions that looked like beehives and had been designed by a local man to keep the midges at bay. They were made of green netting over a supporting wire cage. Don and I each put one on to upstage the coolie hat.

'Oh, my goodness,' spluttered Tish. 'We must have a shot of this.' We cavorted around in our weird field costumes but I don't think she ever used the sequence. And that was the last of the filming.

TWELVE

An End and a Beginning

IT WAS EARLY in March. We had spent a mild winter watching plenty of the usual otter activity but, so far, there had been no sign that either of the two bitches was in her holt with a new generation of cubs. Now, after a gap of several weeks, we were back at Loch Dorran to check.

The snow had come at last and our otter world was contained within an unsullied stillness. Down at the Rock Point watch place we were experiencing the usual wish-we-had-never-been-away feelings. Were Bodach, Pinknose and Palethroat safe? If there were no new cubs, was the pattern of the last five years changed and, if so, why? What were the cubs of last season doing? Were they still tolerated by the dominant dog? Did they still have contact with their mothers? We gloomily scanned a totally calm loch for the answers to these questions, but lacking otters, it reflected only the frozen white wilderness around it and told us nothing.

As so often happened, a sudden brief distraction helped to lift our despondency and keep our interest alive. A family of ravens, which we had often seen in the daytime pottering around on the ridge opposite, rose into the air with indignant cries of 'cruk, cruk, cruk' and came sweeping across the loch towards us. Automatically, binoculars were seized.

We were just in time to see an eaglet, dark in speckled feathering, lifting off from a pinnacle rock on the snowclad ridge and gliding smoothly into the frosty air. Its talons held a lump of newly torn turf, a strange burden which the bird dropped at

once. Then, as a stone might fall from the heavens, wings tight-closed, talons drawn up, head and neck stretched to the limit, the young bird was streaking after it.

The eaglet stooped towards the forest below at breakneck speed, past lowering cliff, shadowed gully and snow-covered ledges, as if bent on sudden death. At the last possible moment, and with barely enough room for manoeuvre, it swooped past its quarry, rose up to meet it and then caught it neatly in its foot. Soaring effortlessly upwards again, no pause in its flight, the youngster drew level with the ridge, rose up and over in a graceful arc, then once more released its soil-encrusted bundle of roots and grass and was hurtling after it to catch and carry again.

The game continued as if the bird would never tire of it – a young eagle perfecting the art of catching its prey. We stood at Rock Point totally absorbed in a demonstration of consummate skill and breathtaking beauty. But it had to end. After the fifth or sixth successful attempt, the young bird at last grew tired. It dropped its imaginary prey without a downward glance, and did not follow after it. Instead it flew further along the crag and alighted on another rock pinnacle. There it began to preen.

'Right,' said Don briskly, after we had decided the bird would stay put for a while. 'I'm off to Badger Point. Be in touch.'

It was a good thing he had whispered, for we were now going to discover our first otter. Two, in fact.

'Hold on,' I said hurriedly.

A couple of brown backs, small humps with no heads or tails, were suddenly visible on the far side of the nearest rocky islet below us. The rocks shelved steeply into the loch there, effectively obscuring sight of the whole of the animals. Undoubtedly, though, two otters were slowly walking over the seaweed, one behind the other, from right to left. The first hump came to a halt. The second caught up and halted too. Then both sank out of sight. Not for the first time we debated whether we should move cautiously to a new position so that we could better observe what was going on or stay where we were and hope the animals would eventually move towards us. We settled for the latter.

Two broad-based tails, tapering to a whiplike end, flew through the air, this way, that way, froze a moment, then

dropped out of sight again. There were angry squeaks. One otter body, still apparently headless, ran forward but was immediately caught by the other. More squabbling. All was made plain when Palethroat appeared from behind a tangle-draped boulder, dragging along a large, flapping lumpsucker. Caorunn, her cub of last season, was doing his best to grab titbits for himself.

The bitch dropped the fish in a small hollow on the rock and they got to work – chomping jaws, crunching teeth, each head lifting to chew and swallow, immense satisfaction written all over their faces. This was a beautiful close-up of these two and gave us a good opportunity to judge their condition. Caorunn had grown into a fine fellow, now between fourteen and fifteen months old, with the typically broad head and the powerful body of a male. He was not far short of the size of his mother but had not inherited her very pale throat and breast. Since it was most unlikely she would be sharing a fish with her sub-adult cub if already she had babes in one of the holts, I tried to imagine her pregnant with the next lot instead, but did not succeed. She did, however, look in excellent health.

On the rocks below, there continued a great tearing and chewing on the red-bellied fish. There was no serious quarrelling now for there was plenty for both. Palethroat soon gave up. Without waiting to groom her coat or wipe her chin and cheeks clean, she dropped the mouthful she was working on, then toddled over the weed and down to the water. There she slipped in, dived, surfaced again and swam out of sight behind Rock Point. Caorunn continued with his succulent meal, appearing not even to notice his mother's departure.

A long pale grey neck, topped by a crested head, calculating eye and wicked sword bill, poked itself above the rocks on the far side of the same skerry rock. A heron. The bird must have been concealed there all the time, for it had certainly not just flown in. It stood, quite still, not looking at the water below, as might have been expected, but in the direction of Caorunn. It seemed to be deeply interested. Then it began to stalk slowly over the rock, the same route the otters had taken, eventually coming to a halt only a few feet behind the preoccupied youngster. There it stayed, solemnly gazing down, as if working out what might be attempted next.

I did not really expect it to do anything, for as far as I knew herons did not eat lumpsuckers of any size, and had no quarrel with otters either. Yet there followed an amusing episode which had us both convulsed with suppressed laughter.

Caorunn remained completely unaware of, or maybe un-impressed by, the deeply engrossed bird and continued with his meal. The heron came to a sudden decision. It turned to the right, then commenced a solemn peregrination right round the busily eating otter, each step a deliberate pace forward, followed by a pause, during which it turned its head to observe what was going on. Back at base, it came to a halt, contemplated the young otter with a serious, speculative air, then set off again on another promenade around it.

This extraordinary bird continued to strut round the otter cub, in ever-decreasing circles, until the distance between it and the fish was no more than a stretching of a long heron neck. Then, hey presto, the head darted forward and a razor-sharp bill speared a large piece of lumpsucker. Taken completely by surprise, Caorunn leapt back, snarling. The bird dropped its prize and, temporarily discomfited, withdrew. The otter ran forward to secure the fish. The bird, not unduly concerned by its failure, recommenced its anti-clockwise marching.

We had been so absorbed in these antics that we had not noticed Palethroat. Suddenly she was emerging through the seaweed in the shallows below and climbing the rock again. She had brought a large eel to share with her cub and her arrival was the perfect distraction for the heron. Predictably, Caorunn abandoned the lumpsucker, ran over to see what his mother had brought, and promptly started squabbling for a share of the eel. The big bird hopped clumsily forward, seized a large portion of the discarded fish in its bill, then stood quite still, looking rather surprised.

At last it made up its mind. There began a comical attempt on the part of an extremely frustrated heron to swallow an impos-sible beakful. The piece of fish was about the size of two tennis balls and bulged out by at least two inches on either side of the slender bill. Up went the head, long neck stretching to the limit, bill pointing to the skies, and then began an energetic attempt to shake it down. After much effort, the awkward lump was safely

in the gullet. Now it had to be persuaded down. The heron stood motionless, a comic look of puzzlement spreading over its face. Then, strength gathered together, once more it tried to swallow. Gulp. *Gulp*. No use. Gulp. GULP. Pause for rest. Gulp, gulp, gargle. Try again. Elastic neck as long as it could be, a frantic look appearing in the heron's eye, this amazing bird continued the effort. Gulp, *gulp*, GULP! Success of a sort. The lump slid down a few inches.

There was really no way that large piece of lumpsucker was ever going to reach the heron's stomach. In the end, it acknowledged defeat.

Defeat, all the same, brought another problem. How to get rid of the most uncomfortable object halfway down its gullet? Staggering all over the slippery weed, its feet sliding drunkenly this way and that, the heron tried in vain to regurgitate its unfortunate meal. Again and again it tried. A distinctly demented look appeared in the creature's eyes, and we became so alarmed for the wretched bird that we even considered the wholly impractical course of going to its rescue.

At last it was done. With a great contortion of the neck and its bill wide open, the heron coughed up the obstruction with a rasping sound. It stood, bewildered and dazed, regarding the nasty mess at its feet and did not immediately fly away from the scene of its discomfiture. We wondered if it had damaged itself.

Meantime, Palethroat and Caorunn, who had been unimpressed by all this carry-on so close to them, were coming to the end of the eel. As the heron stood bemused, they wiped their chins and cheeks and then began a gradual progress over the seaweed down to the loch. After a final sprainting by Palethroat, the action faithfully copied by her son, the two of them were slipping into the loch. They dived and then, one behind the other, Palethroat leading, began to swim for Mallard Bay.

'I'd better go,' whispered Don, and with a final look at the departing otters, he turned back into the wood. He would walk on towards Badger Point and perhaps beyond.

Palethroat and Caorunn duly arrived on the shore in Mallard Bay, just to the east of Otter Point, shook out their coats and began a meticulous grooming. What did that heron do? It stood watching the otters cross the Narrows and then, as soon as they

were safely on the rocks on the other side, launched itself into the air with a wild flapping of its great grey wings, flew over the channel, and alighted on a boulder not far away from them. It stalked carefully through shallow water towards the busy animals and came to a halt only a few feet away. There it stood, quite still, solemnly regarding them. Waiting for what, I wondered. Was this most peculiar heron in need of a heron psychiatrist?

Mother and son finished cleaning-up operations and returned to the water. As I watched them steadily making their way across the bay towards Birch Point, I took an occasional look at the young eagle on the cliffs above. Against a ridge mantled in white and streaked with gold from the risen sun, it was still busily preening its feathers. This was a young golden eagle, and with both golden and white-tailed eagles now seen in the area I wondered if soon they would be competing for living space.

The young eagle lifted off its perch just as Palethroat and Caorunn ran up a cleft in the rock of Birch Point, presumably on their way to a holt. It glided slowly along the crags, landed on a small ledge with an overhang and strutted out of sight into a shadowed cavity free of snow.

I now had time to look around. The Narrows, not yet caught by the sun, were dark and utterly still. The iced-over waters at the head of the loch were held in frozen tranquillity, dotted here and there with snow-covered rocks and seaweed. The outer loch, already in sunshine, was deepest blue and sparkling. It had been a strange winter. Short periods of frost had seemed, each time, the start of a really cold spell which never actually materialised, but now, when there was already a faint flush on the larch and we could almost smell spring in the air, the snow had fallen at last.

The tide was ebbing and already carpets of glistening brown, orange and green seaweed were fringed by rough rocks and boulders all decorated in white. On one side conifer Christmas trees, heavily laden in pristine snow, were bowing and bending with their burdens. On the other, gnarled old oak, birch and rowan trees were glowing in the warming sun and dropping their thawing canopies to the ground. The little world of Loch Dorran, held now in a moment of stillness, would not have long to await the spring.

I thought about Palethroat and Caorunn. The two of them seemed closely tied, so it was almost certain there were no new cubs. If Pinknose, too, was still with her cubs of last year, Coll and Cuan, then the breeding pattern of the past five years was indeed changed. By now Bodach should have been regularly patrolling his territory for intruding males, carefully investigating the scents on all the rock points and duly leaving his own spraint messages to be interpreted. Instead he was keeping a low profile, foraging for long periods, often curling up on the rocks to sleep, and generally behaving as if there were no special pressures in his little world to bother him. Certainly Caorunn would not have been tolerated in this part of the range had there been new families. But the dominant dog was getting on in years, especially for an otter in the wild. Perhaps he was the reason why all was not as usual.

Thoughts of Bodach must have done the trick! The radio crackled quietly and Don spoke.

'Do you read me?'

'Sure.'

'I have Bodach here in Badger Bay. He came from further down the loch and I think he's been in a scrap!'

'What's happened?'

'It looks as if his nose has been bitten.'

I was about to ask for more details when a small movement among the willow scrub fringing Otter Bay caught my eye.

'Hold on. Something's happening here. I'll come back to you.'

It was no more than a flurry of snow falling from a branch of scrub willow. There seemed no good reason for it. The air was as still as the water in the loch, and the bay in deep shadow, untouched as yet by the thawing warmth of the sun. The small disturbance turned out to be an otter. It was pushing aside the vegetation close to the old drain which was a path, often used by otters, to and from a holt in the forest. Now it stood in the gloom of the entrance, carefully scenting and looking out over the loch. Then I realised there were two. Another was standing close behind and to one side.

Seconds later, the two otters decided it was safe to proceed and came leaping and scrambling over the rocks towards the loch. Wildly out of control, they skidded over patches of snow,

spread-eagled down the frozen sides of an almost sheer rock and, on the seaweed below, stumbled, picked themselves up again, shook their heads – no doubt with surprise at the strangeness of the frozen white world about them – and at last reached the water. The impetuous pair, Coll and Cuan, ran straight in and began the inevitable game when two or more otters are gathered together, brisk, energetic and tough. In an exploding fountain of foaming droplets I caught glimpses of thick brown fur, boxing paws, bristling whiskers and snapping teeth.

In only a minute or two they got down to the more serious business of foraging. I thought they seemed likely to stay where they were for some time, for they were catching plenty. It was a good moment in which to contact Don.

'I have Coll and Cuan foraging in Otter Bay. No sign of Pinknose still. What's Bodach doing?'

'He's foraging mid-channel but seems to be gradually making towards Seal Island. I haven't seen Pinknose either.'

'Okay, I'll keep watching. Perhaps Bodach will meet up with the cubs here.'

It was perhaps significant to note how closely tied the two siblings still were, never far apart, the little female always swimming to join the young male whenever the distance between them grew too great. Twice, when one went ashore to eat a fish, the other soon discovered its absence and began 'peeping' pathetically. Eventually they would discover each other again and have a short greetings ceremony before carrying on with foraging or eating. I felt sure that, had Pinknose been in the holt from which they'd come, she would certainly have been with them now. Perhaps, after all, she had a new young family somewhere else. Again the nagging thought – if that were the case, why was Bodach not acting differently? Oh, well. We would have to wait and see.

Apart from foraging cubs, entertainment for the moment was provided by three seals, cumbersome and dark against the rugged white backdrop of Seal Island, humping themselves over the rock to catch the last of the ebbing tide, and a pair of oystercatchers, handsome in black and white with orange dagger bills, working the weed on the skerry rocks below me. A robin scolded somewhere in the wood behind and a rock pipit cheeped

plaintively as it fluttered from snow-covered boulders on to glistening seaweed, hoping for an insect or two. No sign now of the eaglet.

A sudden commotion in the centre of the Narrows between Rock Point and Otter Point alerted me. Was it an otter? Unlikely – it was too great a disturbance. A seal? Not enough water, surely. A gleaming flash of silver broke the surface, rose a couple of feet into the air and porpoised gracefully in an arc towards Mallard Bay. A magnificent salmon. In hot pursuit came a furiously diving and swimming young otter. It was Coll, and the cheeky fellow hadn't a hope, of course.

The salmon smacked down into the water, sank briefly out of sight, then, once more came leaping urgently forward. There was one further glimpse of the quicksilver fish and an ever-hopeful streak of an otter. Then it was all over. The salmon did not surface again and Coll, maybe having come to his senses, broke away and swam back towards his sister. He did not look in the least ruffled, and anyway, it had just been a piece of otter fun.

The young male did not stay foraging beside Cuan but swam and dived onwards towards Marten Bay. The last I saw of him he was rounding Rock Point. In due course, Don would be able to give me news of him.

'Can you see Coll?' I radio'd. 'He swam round into Marten Bay, I think. Cuan is still with me.'

'I've got him all right. Listen to this.' He sounded quite excited. 'Bodach has just gone ashore on the west side of Seal Island and he's chasing an otter. It's not a youngster and I'm almost certain it's Pinknose!'

'So that's where she is! Are you coming up here?' Having found the missing bitch at last, he would not want to miss any interesting action.

'I think so. I'll stop at Marten Point on the way and check on Coll.'

Half an hour later Cuan caught a large lumpsucker right in the centre of the Narrows. Coll was still foraging in Marten Bay. I watched the young female making valiantly for the skerry rocks below me, with the wildly flapping creature held in her mouth. She shallow-dived into the tangle and with a great effort dragged her fish on to the rock. No mean feat. I listened to savage and

satisfied crunching as she set to work on bone and succulent flesh, and admired her plump and obviously excellent condition. The sub-adults must be doing well.

Cuan stopped eating. A forepaw secured her prey to the rock and up came her head to scent. She was looking intently out into the Narrows where something had her complete attention. Now I could hear a call, an inquiring 'peeping': where are you? I'm coming. Another otter. Cuan responded at once with a friendly whickering sound.

It was Coll who came paddling round Rock Point in barely enough water for swimming. He scrambled out on to the rocks and ran to join his sister. The usual ecstatic greetings took place, then the young male, instead of trying to grab a share of the not inconsiderable remains of his sister's fish, took to the water again and began to swim and dive, this time in deeper water, back towards Marten Bay.

I contacted Don at once. 'Can you see Coll from where you are? He's on his way back into Marten Bay, I think.'

'I've got him all right.' Don chuckled. 'For some reason he left a very large lumpsucker on the shore and disappeared in your direction. I can see him now. Looks like he's coming back to his fish. Hey, what's this? He's picking it up and taking it into the water!'

'Looks interesting,' I said with feminine instinct that something unusual might be about to take place. 'Cuan hasn't moved. Be back to you.'

Coll appeared again, paddling in the shallow water at the base of Rock Point, and he certainly had a fish in his mouth – I could see the bright skin of its belly. He dived, popped up only a few feet from his sister, then dragged the remains of his lumpsucker on to the seaweed beside her. There were no greetings this time. He just got down to tearing and eating his fish while she continued placidly with her own. Two sibling otter cubs, companionably together, eating each its own fish and not squabbling. In fact, they took no notice whatever of one another.

This little episode demonstrated once again how closely siblings are tied. From birth they seem automatically to do everything together and dislike being apart. These two were now thirteen or fourteen months old and perhaps separating from

their mother Pinknose, yet they remained as closely tied together as ever. This bonding is extremely strong, and we often saw sub-adults at least two years old still acting in unison. Once maturity is approaching, at around three years, they operate more and more apart.

The process of breaking away from the maternal influence is a slow one, even when new sets of cubs have been born and are still in the holt. Though the mother no longer feeds with the young sub-adults, or lingers long in their company, whenever she meets up with them there are brief but entirely friendly greetings. If, for some reason, the bitch has not bred new cubs, then the family remains closely tied for much longer. We have noted sub-adults as old as two years still with their mother.

In this connection, the crucial period for male sub-adults is when they are close to maturity and soon able to breed. They are, as it were, competitive with their father and therefore creatures to be seen-off to the peripheries of his range. It is then that we see them more and more in the outer loch, very seldom on the inner reaches, and eventually vanishing altogether. Have they found a vacant niche for themselves elsewhere and taken over from another dog, now no longer able to defend his territory? Or have they perished from cause unknown? We would love to know.

Female sub-adults seem to be around much longer and are often to be found in family groups that contain their mothers and new young cubs. We have never seen any evidence of more than two bitches breeding on the range and assume, therefore, that these young females are not mated even when they reach maturity. In due course one may replace a mother who is too old to breed or who has disappeared for whatever reason. Twice we have seen this happen.

Sub-adults Coll and Cuan took another fifteen minutes to finish off their fish. Otters have enormous appetites, perhaps because they may spend long periods in their holts without food, but now even this growing pair seemed to be defeated. Both stood yawning beside the remaining scraps of their monster fishes, and already two predatory gulls had alighted on a rock close by and were waiting to collect.

The twins gave themselves a perfunctory cleaning-up, yawned

again, then slipped into the water and set off for Otter Point. They ran over its great snowclad rocks down into Otter Bay and back to the drain from which they had emerged. The last I saw of them was two fair-sized otter haunches with long tapering tails flowing out behind, vanishing into its all-enveloping gloom. Time to curl somewhere safe and have a sleep.

Don called me to say he was on his way to Rock Point. While waiting, I spent some time checking for Bodach and Pinknose on the skerries and seaweed over at Seal Island. There was no sign of them at all. The little bays between the island and Otter Point were also a blank. In fact our otter world rested in the slack of the tide and it would be most unlikely we would see any more action until it had been rising again an hour or so.

I thought about the young sub-adults, the impetuous Coll, the more sedate Caorunn and the timid little female, Cuan. What was the future for each of them? Coll or Caorunn might eventually succeed the ageing Bodach, though there were probably other males about who would compete. Cuan might replace one of the females. It was the previous five years of successful breeding, fifteen cubs in all, which started me mulling over a problem which always fascinated us. There seemed to be no more otters on the loch than usual! What happened to the surplus?

It was reasonable to assume that natural wastage must account for some, animals dying from disease, or from injuries in fights or from road or marine accidents. There would also be animals not able to support themselves and eventually dying. Others would look for new ranges. Probably all these factors were relevant. One frustration of the study was that, though we could be sure, eventually, that a certain animal was no longer present on the range, we could do no more than guess the reason why.

From time to time we discovered dead otters, usually near the shore, almost always youngsters and with a bias towards males. On two occasions we had the dead bodies analysed for cause of death. A young male with a badly bitten nose – youngsters fighting or a scrap with the dominant male perhaps – had died from a wound that turned septic. Another had died from a blow to the head, possibly a kick from one of two ponies grazing near the shore. Young otters are notoriously inquisitive.

Don came softly from the wood behind me.

'Anything doing?' he whispered.

I shook my head.

'Are you cold? If possible, I think we should wait another hour or so, till the tide is running. The light should be good for a while.'

It certainly was bitterly cold and clear skies above promised a fairly hard frost. Nevertheless, it was always magic at Rock Point – unless it was pouring buckets and a stiff wind from a northerly direction was blowing, then it could be awful – and it was never boring. It was particularly lovely when few, if any, other folk were about, the deep silence on a still day broken only by elements of the natural world. Then the gentle lapping of a newly rising tide against the giant rocks below would whisper of exciting happenings to come. Ravens might speak gruffly to each other in the heavens above. Great torpedo bodies would glide quietly by and the sad eyes of seals turn to examine our rock. Little birds would whistle to each other in the wood behind. Great stuff!

In mid-afternoon, on this March day, rough-hewn crags were starkly etched against snow-covered ridges. Ten red deer hinds in a long straggling line were daintily picking their way over the unsullied heights to forest shelter below. Mist was forming over the serene waters of the Narrows, sure sign of a cold night to follow. A cormorant was fishing. So clear was the water that we could see its black, elongated shape, neck stretched and wings held close to its body, stroking its way to the bottom. Tendrils in the seaweed forest were all languidly leaning with the stirrings of the tide, bending to its gentle commands. Five herons flew in one by one on ponderously flapping wings to take up stances along the shore. Grumpy-looking, but patient, they waited for what the tide would bring. The rowans on the top of Seal Island were picked out in gold by the setting sun.

And the tide was indeed moving in. It began to chuckle against the great granite rock beneath us and climb imperceptibly over the tangle on the skerry rocks. Eddies began to form on the smooth surface of the water, ruffling its stillness and beginning to sweep ever more urgently along. Soon they were whirling and swirling in a myriad of rippling circles, all hurrying and scurrying through the Narrows to spread themselves out in the breadth of

the loch beneath Ben Dorain. The waters of the Narrows, utterly still and at peace in the last of the day, had become an irresistable force whisking all, helpless, along with it.

Urgency was in the air too. Suddenly from the other side of Rock Point a compelling call pierced the sound of the rushing waters. From Otter Point an excited whickering replied. A large otter came running out of the little conifer wood on its top, bounding over the snow-covered rocks, scrambling ungracefully downwards over ice-clad rock sides and razor-sharp edges, leaping clumsily over cracks and crevices. It skidded over the seaweed, legs spreadeagling every whichway, arrived at the water's edge and, with no hesitation at all, plunged in. Bodach! I noted his injured nose.

Sweeping round from Marten Bay came another otter – Pinknose! She came gliding along on the rising tide, dark head cleaving the surface, long body and tapering tail stretching out behind. Calm eyes glanced briefly up the sheer sides of Rock Point, giving us a glimpse of a distinctive pink nose, then turned away and continued on.

Both dived at almost the same moment, then came together in the seaweed forest below, tails a-flicking, feet a-kicking, supple bodies twisting and turning in and out of the tangle weed. They rose up through the water, grey muzzle to sleek, young muzzle, boxing and biting, whickering at the tops of their voices and churning the Narrows into a cauldron of bubbling white water. A joyous greeting.

Pinknose rolled languidly over and Bodach swam swiftly to join her, rolling over too. Then, side by side, they floated through the Narrows, whirling and swirling on the eddying tide, tails first, feet in air, heads turned to watch each other, in perfect harmony of movement. Past Otter Point they swept, rolling and bowling along on the urgent waters and arrived, unresisting, in the quiet of Mallard Bay.

They righted themselves and immediately the bitch streamed away: catch-me-if-you-can, let's have some fun. Provocative, and swift in this watery element as a swallow in the air, she headed down into the tangle, weaving in and out of the gently undulating tendrils, swerving, curving, infinitely desirable and quite uncatchable.

Her scent was strong in the water and Bodach was deeply roused. With a flick of his tail, hind feet kicking, forelegs held tight to his chest, he sped after his elusive mate. Little bitch here, little bitch there. Bitch inviting, bitch enticing, her sinuous body teasing, tormenting, never quite caught, but wanting to be caught. Corkscrewing, chittering, chattering, somersaulting, squealing, the impetuous pair continued their courtship for several minutes. The climax was reached at last. Bodach grabbed and held his submissive mate by the scruff, wrapped his forelegs round her sides, and mounted her surely. She sank beneath his thrusting body and only their heads broke the surface, as they bobbed up and down in the waters of Mallard Bay.

The pair broke apart in only a couple of minutes. They dived shallow into the weed, rose again, whickering excitedly, and scrambled out on to the rocks of Otter Point. Thick dark coats all spiky and clinging, were shaken out and then Pinknose, with an inviting little chirrup, led away. Off they went, stumbling from one slippery boulder to another, right to the top of the great rock outcrop, streaking through secret little tunnels in the snowy heather, and in and out of the dark young conifer trees.

For five minutes they continued their mad romp and then they were tumbling, helter skelter for the water. The courtship game was played once more, and they mated again. When they came ashore we could see the excitement was over at last. They glided soberly in, at peace together, hauled out on to the rocks and began to groom side by side on the seaweed. A final shaking out and thick fur coats, sleek and shining in the last of the golden light, fell into place. Both otters were yawning. Pinknose climbed higher on the rock to a small hollow in the bracken, clear of snow, and curled tightly on the rust red bed. Moments later Bodach joined her. He settled against her silky body, stretching his head over her soft neck. Then both were sleeping.

Half an hour later this amorous pair went their separate ways. Pinknose pottered down to the loch and into Otter Bay. She dived, popped up again, and began to swim towards Seal Island. Quite soon she vanished into the gloom. Bodach wandered about for a little while, sniffing the rock and golden brown seaweed. He seemed in no great hurry. Perhaps, at last, he was tired.

Eventually he dropped a spraint, trundled down to the water, and breasted in.

We watched old Bodach, majestic as ever, slowly paddling in the direction of Birch Point. He did not forage but now and again paused in his swimming to float on the water, forepaws paddling gently, wise eyes in broad grizzled head slowly inspecting the shore, long body at rest, tail flowing out behind. Then he continued on his way. Patrolling? In due course he ran over the rocks at Birch Point and disappeared into the trees.

We stretched cold and cramped limbs, not noticed till this moment when the exciting action was over, packed up our rucksacks and began the long tramp back through the ancient oak woods to the caravan. Dirk and Shian, Calum Cat and The Golden Wonder would all be there and waiting for us.

Epilogue

Twin cubs were born to Pinknose in the early part of June, a delightful new Coll and Cuan who arrived on the shore in mid-September. Palethroat did not produce a family. She and Caorunn remained together well on into the autumn. The three sub-adult cubs, now called Caorunn and the Heavenly Twins, often met together in the outer loch for the usual tempestuous games. Alas, we never saw friend Bodach again.

What is the future for the otter? Naturalists over the whole of its range are concerned for its welfare. Surveys have been done to check on its status and no doubt will continue to be done. The general public, those of them interested in wildlife and conservation, are also beginning to be more aware of the plight of many wildlife species. Their concern is vital.

In Britain the otter has the protection of the Wildlife and Countryside Act 1981, but of what use is protecting the animal if it has no suitable habitat wherein to exist? However healthy numbers may be at present, disturbance from people all anxious to enjoy wild coasts and countryside could quite soon be a significant threat. The effects on the otter of the ever-expanding fish-farming business is as yet unknown, but certainly cannot be ignored.

Really, it is up to all of us. If we are concerned enough for the welfare of this enchanting little animal then we will see to it that it survives, and in healthy numbers.

Acknowledgments

Grateful thanks are due to the Wemyss family for their kind cooperation and help over the years; to the Forestry Commission for permission to explore their woods and shores in the interests of the study; to Jim and Rosemary Green of the Vincent Wildlife Trust for useful discussion and information garnered from two otter surveys; to Margaret Grimwade for invaluable back-up observation; to Matthew Wilson for keeping us up to date when we have been absent; and to Jean Edwards for help with checking proofs. Especially I would like to thank Tony Colwell, my editor at Jonathan Cape, for his meticulous attention to the text and much useful advice.

To Mick and Jean Hornsby we owe a special debt of gratitude for friendship over the years and help willingly proffered in moments of difficulty.

Select Bibliography

H. Mortimer Batten, *Habits and Characters of British Wild Animals*, Chambers, London 1920.

H.A. Bryden, *Horn and Hound*, Methuen, London 1927.

Paul Chanin, *The Natural History of Otters*, Croom Helm, London 1985.

P.R.F. Chanin and D.J. Jefferies, 'The decline of the otter Lutra lutra in Britain: an analysis of hunting records and discussion of causes', *Biological Journal of the Linnean Society 10*, London 1978. (p. 305–28).

Alfred Heneage Cocks, 'Notes on the Breeding of the Otter', *Proceedings of the Zoological Society No. XVII*, London 1881. (p. 249–50).

A.K. Crawford, D. Evans, A. Jones and J. McNulty, *Otter Survey of Wales*, Society for the Promotion of Nature Conservation, Lincoln 1979.

F. Fraser Darling, *Natural History in the Highlands and Islands*, Collins, London 1947.

J. Wentworth Day, *British Animals of the Wild Places*, Blandford Press, London 1980.

Lionel Edwards, *The Wiles of the Fox*, Medici Society and Sporting Gallery, London 1932.

——*The Fox*, Collins, London 1949.

K.M. Elliott, 'The otter (Lutra lutra L.) in Spain', *Mammal Review 13*, London 1983. (p. 25–34).

R. Elmhirst, 'Food of the otter in the marine littoral zone', *Scottish Naturalist* 1938. (p. 99–102).

S. Erlinge, 'Home range of the otter Lutra lutra L. in southern Sweden', *Oikos 18*, 1967. (p. 186–209).

M.L. Gorman, D. Jenkins and R.J. Harper, 'The anal scent sacs of the otter (Lutra lutra)', *Journal of the Zoological Society 186*, London 1978. (p. 463–74).

J. Green, 'Sensory perception in hunting otters, Lutra lutra L.', *Otters: Journal of the Otter Trust*, Edinburgh 1977. (p. 13–16).

J. Green and R. Green, *Otter Survey of Scotland 1977–1979*, The Vincent Wildlife Trust, London 1980.

——'The otter (Lutra lutra L.) in western France', *Mammal Review 11*, London 1981. (p. 181–7).

J. Green, R. Green and D.J. Jefferies, 'A radio-tracking survey of otters Lutra lutra (L., 1758) on a Perthshire river system', *Lutra 27*, Gouda (Holland) 1984. (p. 85–145).

C.J. Harris, *Otters: a Study of the Recent Lutrinae*, Weidenfeld and Nicolson, London 1968.

L. Harrison Matthews, *British Mammals*, Collins, London 1952.

V.D. Hawley and F.E. Newby, 'Marten home ranges and population fluctuations', *Journal of Mammalogy 38*, American Society of Mammalogists, 1957. (p. 174–84).

H.R. Hewer, *British Seals*, Collins, London 1974.

R. Hewson, 'Food and feeding habits of otters Lutra lutra at Loch Park, north-east Scotland', *Journal of the Zoological Society 170*, London 1973. (p. 159–62).

H.G. Hurrell, *Wildlife: Tame But Free*, David and Charles, Newton Abbot (Devon) 1968.

H.G. Hurrell, *Foxes*, Sunday Times Publications, London 1962.

D.J. Jefferies, J. Green and R. Green, *Commercial Fish and Crustacean Traps: a Serious Cause of Otter Mortality in Britain and Europe*, The Vincent Wildlife Trust, London 1984.

D. Jenkins, 'Ecology of otters in northern Scotland. I. Otter (Lutra lutra) breeding and dispersion in mid-Deeside, Aberdeenshire, in 1974–79', *Journal of Animal Ecology 49*, Cambridge 1980. (p. 755–74).

D. Jenkins and R.J. Harper, 'Fertility in European otters (Lutra lutra)', *Journal of the Zoological Society 197*, London 1982. (p. 299–300).

D. Jenkins, J.G.K. Walker and D. McCowan, 'Analyses of otter (Lutra lutra) faeces from Deeside, N.E. Scotland', *Journal of the Zoological Society 187*, London 1979. (p. 235–44).

A. King and A. Potter, *A Guide to Otter Conservation for Water Authorities*, The Vincent Wildlife Trust, London 1980.

A. King, J. Ottoway and A. Potter, *The Declining Otter: a guide to its Conservation*, Friends of the Earth, London 1979.

J.E. King, *Seals of the World*, British Museum (Natural History), London 1964.

H. Kruuk and R. Hewson, 'Spacing and foraging of otters (Lutra lutra) in a marine habitat', *Journal of the Zoological Society 185*, London 1978. (p. 200–12).

L. Laidler, *Otters in Britain*, David and Charles, Newton Abbot (Devon) 1982.

E.J. Lenton, P.R.F. Chanin and D.J. Jefferies, *Otter Survey of England 1977–79*, Nature Conservancy Council, London 1980.

Emil E. Liers, 'Notes on the river otter (Lutra canadensis)', *Journal of Mammalogy 32 No. 1*, American Society of Mammalogists 1951. (p. 1–8).

H.G. Lloyd, *The Red Fox*, Batsford, London 1950.

J.D. Lockie, 'The estimation of the food of foxes', *Journal of Wild Life Management, Vol. 23*, Menasha, Wisconsin, U.S.A. 1959.

J.D. Lockie, 'The food of the pine marten (Martes martes) in west Ross-shire, Scotland', *Proceedings of the Zoological Society 136*, London 1961. (p. 187–95).

——'Distribution and fluctuations of the pine marten Martes martes (L.) in Scotland', *Journal of Animal Ecology 33*, Cambridge 1964. (p. 349–56).

Don and Bridget MacCaskill, *Wild Endeavour*, Blackie, Glasgow 1975.

David MacDonald, *Running with the Fox*, Unwin Hyman, London 1987.

D.W. MacDonald, 'On food preference in the red fox', *Mammal Review 7*, London 1977. (p. 7–23).

S.M. MacDonald, 'The status of the otter in the British Isles', *Mammal Review 13*, 1983. (p. 11–23).

C.F. Mason and S.M. MacDonald, *Otters – Ecology and Conservation*, Cambridge University Press, 1986.

M.H. Markley and C.F. Bassett, 'Habits of captive marten', *American Midland Naturalist 28*, Notre Dame, Indiana, U.S.A. (p. 604–16).

Gavin Maxwell, *Ring of Bright Water*, Longman, London 1960.

Hugh Miles, *The Track of the Wild Otter*, Elm Tree Press, London 1984.

A.J. Mitchell-Jones, D.J. Jefferies, J. Twelves, J. Green and R. Green, 'A practical system of tracking otters in Britain using radiotelemetry and 65-ZN', *Lutra 27*, Gouda (Holland) 1984. (p. 71–84).

Ernest Neal, *Otters*, Sunday Times Publications (Animals of Britain No. 8), London 1962.

Oliver G. Pike, *Wild Animals in Britain*, Macmillan, London 1950.

Kenneth W. Richmond, *Wild Animals of Britain*, Oxford University Press 1946.

J. Rowbottom, 'Watching Otters in Scotland', *Animals 12*, London 1969. (p. 159–61).

H.N. Southern and J.S. Watson, 'Summer Food of the Red Fox in Great Britain', *Journal of Animal Ecology Vol. 10*, Cambridge 1941.

David Stephen, *String Lug the Fox*, Lutterworth Press, London 1950.

B.J. Trowbridge, 'Olfactory communications in the European otter Lutra l. Lutra', PhD thesis, University of Aberdeen, 1983.

Brian Vesey-Fitzgerald, *Town Fox Country Fox*, Deutsch, London 1965.

A. Watson, 'The Winter Food of six Highland Foxes', *Scottish Naturalist 67*, 1955.

H. Watson, *Coastal Otters in Shetland*, The Vincent Wildlife Trust, London 1978.

Philip Wayre, *The River People*, Collins, London 1976.

——*The Private Life of the Otter*, Batsford, London 1979.

Gilbert White, *The Natural History of Selborne*, 1979, but many later editions. (Journal, edited by Walter Johnson, 1931).

Henry Williamson, *Tarka the Otter*, Harmsworth, London 1927.

M.H. Wise, 'The feeding ecology of otters and mink in Devon', PhD thesis, University of Exeter, 1978.

J.R. Young, *Fox-hunting*, Longmans Green, London 1934.